M shed

Tangent Books

 BRISTOL BOOKS

Bristol Music: Seven Decades Of Sound
First published 2018 by Tangent Books and Bristol Books CIC

Tangent Books
Unit 5.16 Paintworks, Bristol BS4 3EH
0117 972 0645
www.tangentbooks.co.uk

Bristol Books CIC
The Courtyard, Wraxall Hill, Bristol BS48 1NA
01275 393933

ISBN: 978-1-910089-75-0

A CIP record of this book is available at the British Library.

Printed on paper from a sustainable source
by Hobbs the Printers Ltd, Totton, Hampshire.

MIX
Paper from
responsible sources
FSC® C020438
www.fsc.org

ACKNOWLEDGEMENTS

This book was published as a partnership between M Shed, Tangent Books and Bristol Books. Thanks to Rebecca Peters and Lee Hutchinson at M Shed; Dr Rehan Hyder at UWE; Clive Burlton, Martin Powell and Joe Burt at Bristol Books

Writing, research, production credits

Alexi Hamilton-King, Mike Tobin, Gill Loats, Chris Burton, Mike Darby/Bristol Archive Records, Gil Gillespie, Mike Crawford, Thomas Brooman, Tony Bullimore, Simon Harding, Clive Burlton and the many people who contributed to the research carried out by the M Shed curators

Picture, design and illustration credits

Front cover logo design and flap typography: Felix Braun

Book design and typography: Joe Burt, Wild Spark Design

Front cover flap picture: Enterprise Sound System, St Paul's Carnival, July, 1985 by Beezer

Back cover flap picture: Alastair Shuttleworth/LICE, Louisiana, May 2017 by Simon Holliday

P4 *Western Scene* loaned by Mike Tobin; P6 Poster loaned by Bristol Archive Records; P10-11 *Western Scene* loaned by Mike Tobin; P28-29: Image loaned by Ian A Anderson; P34 Poster loaned by Mike Tobin; P38 Image loaned by Bristol Books CIC; P45, P53, P60, P68-69, P75, P84 Image loaned by Tangent Books; P101 Mark Stewart and Gareth Sager of the Pop Group, Alexandra Palace, London, June 1980 by Paul Roberts; P107, P112 Image loaned by Tangent Books; P120 Tricky, Kensal Rise, London, 1989 by Beezer

WESTERN SCENE

Volume I No. 1 | Saturday, August 24th, 1963 | Fortnightly | Price SIXPENCE

THE WEST'S ONE AND ONLY ENTERTAINMENTS PAPER

Johnny Carr and The Cadillacs   Photo: Dezo Hoffmann

The first issue of *Western Scene*.

CONTENTS

Live music on Park Street in 1977.

INTRODUCTION

• • • • • •

Welcome to *Bristol Music: Seven Decades of Sound*, the book that accompanies the 2018 exhibition of the same name at M Shed, Bristol.

One of the questions that the exhibition curators asked the musicians, promoters, DJs, fans, authors and others with whom they consulted when researching the exhibition was 'What makes Bristol music special?'

Of course, they got different answers from different people, but one of the themes that emerged was that Bristol music often tends towards the radical and cult rather than the mainstream.

A consequence of this is that Bristol bands have rarely enjoyed prolonged mainstream chart success. Of course, there are exceptions such as Acker Bilk, Russ Conway and David and Jonathan but that was in the late 50s and early-mid 60s. Adge Cutler and Fred Wedlock also represented Bristol in the mainstream charts and, of course, Bananarama and Wayne Hussey have been massively

"Bristol music often tends towards the radical and cult rather than the mainstream."

successful. But Bananarama moved to London and had their big break with the Midlands-based two-tone sound and Hussey's bands were associated with the Leeds and Liverpool goth scene rather than Bristol.

Here's another thing... Bristol is the largest UK city not to have a regular presence in the top flight of the football pyramid. OK, Bristol City were in Division One between 1976-1980, but historically Bristol is not a football city even though (some might argue *because*) it has two teams.

For many years Bristol made little impact on those two essential expressions of working-class culture, football and popular music. It is surely a coincidence that it was in 1976 when City made it into the top flight that things started to change in music as well.

Given the underground nature of a lot of Bristol music, the story of how we got from Russ Conway to Massive Attack is not well documented. The M Shed exhibition is designed to encourage people to tell their stories and will act as a great opportunity to gather the artefacts and personal accounts to assist in the telling of that story.

This book falls into three sections – images of some of the artefacts gathered by M Shed's curators, a timeline and an extensive but far from definitive list of some of the key artists over the last seven decades.

"The story of how we got from Russ Conway to Massive Attack is not well documented."

One of the key years in that timeline is 1976. That's when prog rockers Stackridge played a farewell gig, punk bands the Cortinas and the Primates and reggae outfit Revelation Rockers formed. There's a real sense of change in 1976 which is reinforced in 1977 by the Cortinas releasing their first singles and the arrival of the Pop Group.

From there we can see a lineage to Wild Bunch, Smith &
Mighty and eventually to Massive Attack and the release of
Blue Lines in 1991. And we can then see the influence of *Blue
Lines* on Portishead, Tricky, Roni Size & Reprazent and others.

Of course, you may have a different experience of Bristol
music so come along to the M Shed exhibition and share it.
And enjoy the book.

Richard Jones

POPULAR

Johnny Carr W

WARREN DAVIES — WINNER OF THE D.J. SECTION.

Three cheers and all that to Johnny Carr and his great backing group, the Cadillacs, for winning The Western Scene Popularity Poll for the third year running. Johnny Carr was also placed first in sections 3 and 4. The Force Wild who last year fell to second at all, were placed second in the Cadillacs in section four, and Danny Clarke also second to Johnny Carr in section 7. Pete Budd and The Rebels have won section 5 for the third year running, so congratulations to you boys.

Several groups on the favourites with the Yardpoll who did not get birds and Manfred Mann too placed last year including in their book. There were The Roadrunners, Starbeats, Winners who include the Devils, Concords, Franklin Amen Corner and Bandsplay, the Star Penguins. This is hear the Atlantics and the quite likely that in the last Bluesplay. It is a large that at least 10 groups who quantity in the first hand have been placed this year section.

At the Beatles first not Chris Barlowe association placed, a blow to me. Were in with the Avas Clan, has the past, but The Wests are once again topped both our indebted to the poll, to the female section, with new remarkable such useful place comers Joanne and Samantha. The Rolling Stones who dear rating very good and very and surprise. Vickie has a gorgeous young lady from Denmark has done very well even though she has only sung in Brazil once.

Last year we noted the number of stars that group over in Germany had so slumped in this year we added a section. Favourite group who had moved ahead in the past year. Last year we said how the Vikings had done and sure enough they are still as popular as ever, placing this by winning this section. Colin Anthony, the Jagulars and Casey Jones and the Governors following very close.

Biggest shock this year was to see that last year's favourites, Cole Young and the Graduates had not got many votes. I wonder why.

THE STONES, second last year, first this year in Visiting National Attraction Section.

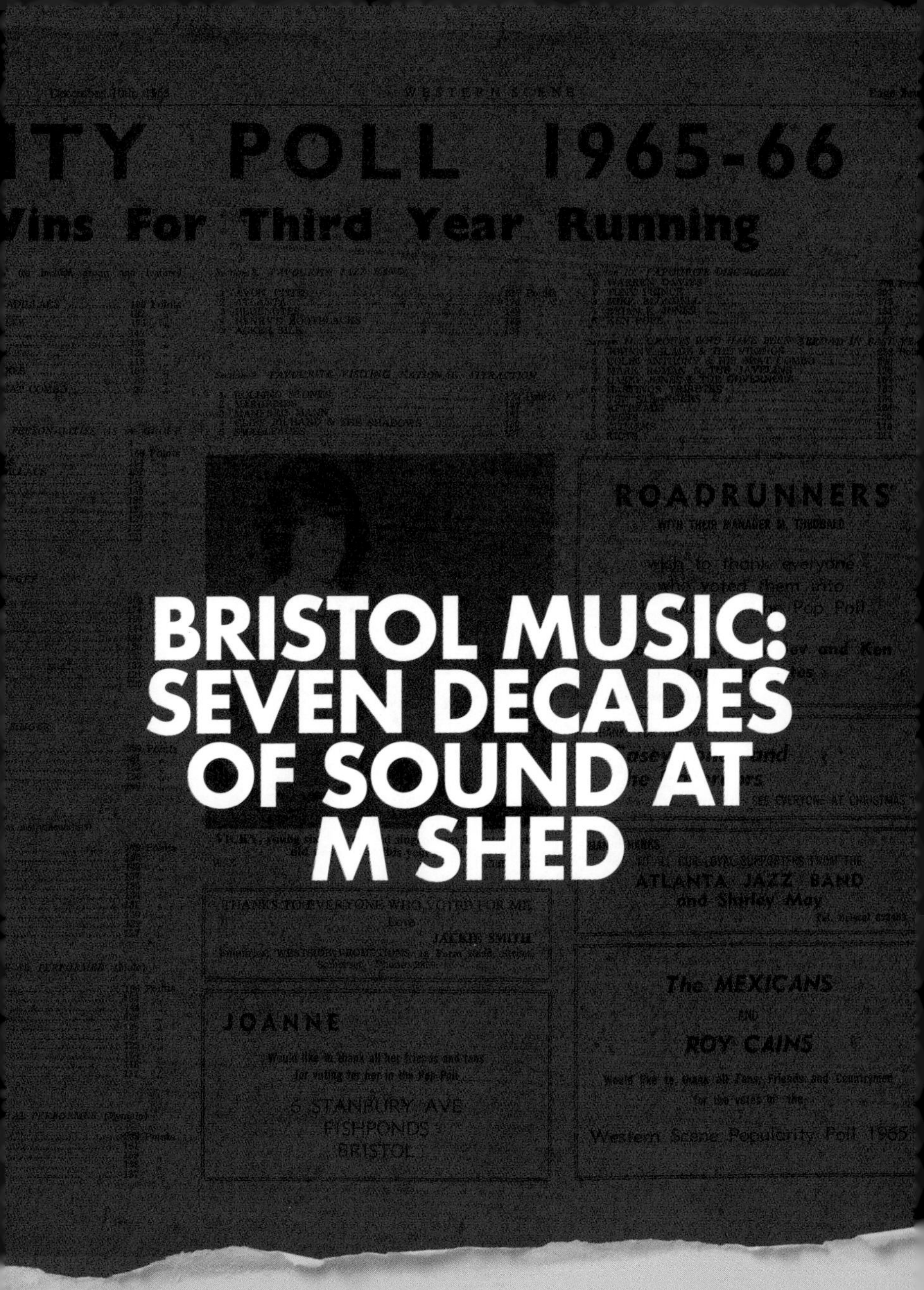

...TY POLL 1965-66

...ins For Third Year Running

ROADRUNNERS
WITH THEIR MANAGER M. THURBRED

BRISTOL MUSIC: SEVEN DECADES OF SOUND AT M SHED

SEE EVERYONE AT CHRISTMAS

ATLANTA JAZZ BAND
and Shirley May

THANKS TO EVERYONE WHO VOTED FOR ME

JACKIE SMITH

JOANNE

6 STANBURY AVE
FISHPONDS
BRISTOL

The MEXICANS
and
ROY CAINS

Western Scene Popularity Poll 1965

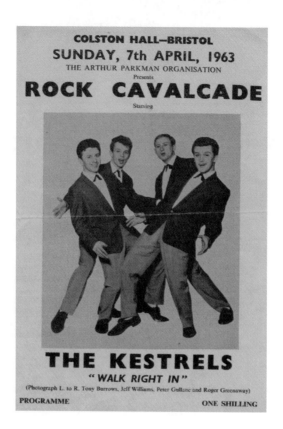

COLSTON HALL POSTER
1963 | LOANED BY MIKE TOBIN

The Kestrels formed in 1955. The vocal harmony quartet were one of Bristol's most popular groups and included Roger Greenaway (pictured far right) who went on to have top 10 hits with Roger Cook as David and Jonathan.

ATLANTIC ROLLERS
MID 60S | LOANED BY BRISTOL ARCHIVES

The Atlantic Rollers were regular performers at the Bamboo Club and were managed by the club owner Tony Bullimore (pictured front). This picture was taken by *Western Scene* photographer Cliff Bulley. The location is probably in front of St Agnes Church.

WILD BUNCH

1986 | LOANED BY TANGENT BOOKS

An unknown photographer captured this iconic image of the Wild Bunch opposite Special K's cafe at the bottom of St Michael's Hill. From left: Grant Marshall (Daddy G), Robert Del Naja (MC 3D), Claude Williams (MC Willy Wee), Nellee Hooper (DJ Nellee), Miles Johnson (DJ Milo).

CARLTON MCCARTHY

1990 | LOANED BY TANGENT BOOKS

This image was sent out with review copies of the *Call Is Strong* LP. The record was an important landmark in what we now recognise as 'The Bristol Sound'. It was produced by Smith & Mighty who also worked with Carlton and a fledgling Massive Attack on the 'Any Love' single.

FOLK AND BLUES POSTER

1967 | LOANED BY IAN A ANDERSON

The folk and blues scene was paticularly vibrant in the 60s and 70s. Venues such as the Troubadour in Clifton and the Stonehouse are most readily associated with folk music, but the Old Duke in King Street also hosted regular sessions.

TROUBADOUR CLUB

1967 | LOANED BY IAN A ANDERSON

Founders Ray and Barbara Willmott outside the Troubadour club on Waterloo Street in Clifton Village. The club opened its doors in October 1966 and became an important hub for the city's folk scene before closing in 1971.

VICE SQUAD

1979 | LOANED BY SIMON EDWARDS

An early picture of Vice Squad who went on to become one of the city's leading punk bands when their single 'Last Rockers' was championed by John Peel and sold more than 20,000 copies. From left: Beki Bondage (vocals), Mark Hambly (bass), Dave Bateman (guitar), Shane Baldwin (drums).

THE CORTINAS

1977 | LOANED BY RACHEL GOODCHILD/STEPHEN SWAN

Credited as being Bristol's first punk band, the Cortinas were still at school when they exploded onto the city scene in 1976. The band were (left to right) Dexter Dalwood (bass), Nick Sheppard (guitar), Mike Fewings (guitar), Jeremy Valentine (vocals), Daniel Swan (drums).

WESTERN STAR POSTER
1987 | LOANED BY STEPHEN WOOD

The Western Star Domino Club was one of Bristol's great venues until it was demolished to make way for a car park at the bottom of the M32. It was a West Indian domino and social club but various promoters put on nights ranging from acid house to punk and in this case, indie, with the Flatmates.

BAMBOO CLUB

LATE 60S | LOANED BY BRISTOL ARCHIVES

Tony and Lalel Bullimore opened the Bamboo Club, Bristol's first West Indian Entertainment Centre, on October 28, 1966. It hosted many famous American and Jamaican artists including Bob Marley and Jimmy Cliff and was also the original headquarters for Bristol West Indian Cricket Club.

RESTRICTION

1983 | LOANED BY BRISTOL ARCHIVE RECORDS

Restriction emerged from the Arts Opportunity Theatre project in St Paul's and although they were only around for a few years and released just one single, several members went on to be influential on the Bristol scene especially guitarist Rob Smith who formed Smith & Mighty with Ray Mighty.

PUNK AT TRINITY

1981 | LOANED BY JOHN FINCH

Trinity hall in Old Market provided an important stage for punk and reggae bands whose audiences were not always welcome in the mainstream city centre venues. This Bristol Punk Festival was organised by Bear Hackenbush, singer with Lunatic Fringe.

ASHTON COURT FESTIVAL '83

OFFICIAL FESTIVAL PROGRAMME 20p

WELCOME to Ashton Court '83, the biggest and best street fair in the West and it's all on grass. This is the 8th free festival at Ashton Court and while the event has had to be reduced to one day this year we are confident that it will be as enjoyable and hassle-free as the previous gatherings.

We've had a lot of fun and not a few headaches getting this showcase for local talent together With two stages, a marquee and an open theatre area, they'll be plenty to keep you occupied during the day. Have a great time and please help us by following a few simple guidelines laid down by the Council:

■ Strictly no camping
■ No fires
■ No motorbikes on site please park in the car park and walk so tht no kids get run over this year

IF THESE RULES ARE BROKEN ASHTON COURT WILL NOT HAPPEN AGAIN
Now relax and start bopping

ASHTON COURT FESTIVAL PROGRAMME
1983 | LOANED BY TANGENT BOOKS

Ashton Court Festival was banned in 1981 following problems with the 1980 event, there wasn't one in 1982 so 1983 was very much a new beginning. *Venue* magazine, and in particular music editor Dave Higgitt, were instrumental in getting the festival up and running again.

CRAZY TRAINS

The raunchiest young rockers in town, Crazy Trains' raw R'n'B has already attracted plenty of media attention plus a well deserved cult following. Vital and refreshing.

RESTRICTION
Formed out of the Arts Opportunity Theatre group last year, this young reggae band have failed to live up to their original promise and are now hampered by the lack of a proper lead singer. Still, their hearts are in the right place and an injection of new blood can only do them good.

BLURT
Lead by the boggled-eyed, mercurial Ted Milton on vocals and sax, this three piece from Stroud play manic dance music with relentless, uncompromising energy.

THE UNTOUCHABLES
Bristol's R'n'B harp prodigy Jerry Tremaine is back in town! Fresh from a world tour with Bad Manners, Jerry will be bringing his youthful brand of stomping blues to Ashton Court with a very special one-off appearance.

ASHTON COURT FESTIVAL PROGRAMME
1983 | LOANED BY TANGENT BOOKS

The one-day event in 1983 was an impressive showcase for Bristol music and performance art. Bands included Startled Insects, Crazy Trains, Blurt, the Untouchables, Restriction, Black Roots and Maximum Joy.

The Burlington Berties

THE BURLINGTON BERTIES

MID 60S | LOANED BY ROWLAND BARTER

Burlington Bertie's Banjo Band released a couple of LPs in 1960 and a further one in 1967. If the gentleman second from the left looks familiar that's because he's better known as DJ Derek. In the 1960s he was the drummer with the Berties and before that with Dave Rivers and The Ramrods.

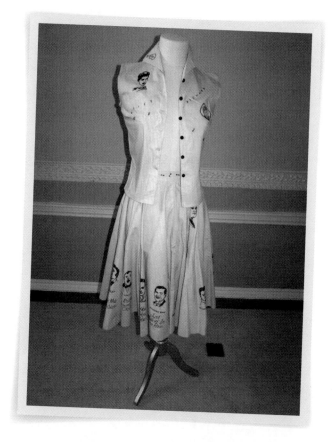

CLIFF RICHARD BLOUSE AND SKIRT
1959 | LOANED BY MARY FLOYDE

Mary Floyde's mother embroidered this outfit with illustrations of Cliff Richard and other rock 'n' roll stars. Fourteen-year-old Mary wore it to the Cliff Richard concert at the Colston Hall on May 6, 1959. She later wore it at St Mark's Church Youth Club, Easton, where it was much admired.

HISTORY OF THE BRISTOL BEAT

1955

▶ Guitarist Pete Creed forms the Red Comets, possibly Bristol's first skiffle group.

▶ Vocal harmony quartet the Kestrels are launched. Members include Roger Greenaway and Tony Burrows, both of whom go on to be hugely successful singers and songwriters.

1956

▶ The Avon Cities Skiffle Group, an offshoot of the long-established Avon Cities Jazz Band, fronted by vocalist Ray Bush, record eight tracks for the Tempo label in June.

1957

▶ Guitarist and singer Al Read begins a weekly Teenagers Live Music Club at The Beeches in Filton, with his Cemetery Skiffle group as resident band.

▶ Pianist Russ Conway records his first single for EMI's Columbia label. 'Party Pops' is a medley of standard songs including 'Roll The Carpet Up' and 'The Westminster Waltz'. It reaches number 24 in the UK Singles Charts.

1958

▶ Buddy Holly And The Crickets play the Colston Hall on March 23.

▶ Bristol bands shed the skiffle craze in favour of rock 'n' roll. Washboards are discarded for drum kits, acoustic guitars swapped for electric and tea chest bass players become bass guitarists.

1959

▶ The Comets (formerly the Red Comets skiffle group, but now a rock 'n' roll band) play at the 'Birthplace Of British Pop Music' the 2i's Coffee Bar in Soho, London.

▶ On October 31, Mike Tobin And The Magnettes become the first Bristol rock 'n' roll band to play at the Colston Hall. The event is a Youth Club Display. Admission is two and sixpence.

▶ Russ Conway knocks 'Smoke Gets In Your Eyes' by The Platters off the top of the charts to claim his first Number One with his self-penned 'Side Saddle'. It is Number One from March 27-April 23 before being replaced by Buddy Holly's 'It Doesn't Matter Anymore'.

▶ On June 19, Russ Conway replaces Elvis Presley at Number One when his piano instrumental 'Roulette' takes the place of 'A Fool Such As I'. It is Number One for two weeks before being replaced by Bobby Darin's 'Dream Lover'.

1960

▶ In April, American stars Eddie Cochran and Gene Vincent appear for a week at the Bristol Hippodrome. Eddie is killed in a car accident near Chippenham on the way back to London.

▶ In December The Comets in conjunction with their Manager Brian K Jones promote the first Groups Galore show at the Colston Hall. Featuring many of the leading local bands and singers the show sells out.

1961

▶ Following the success of the inaugural Groups Galore show the previous year, the event is repeated at the Colston Hall in December with a line up that includes all of the leading Bristol bands and singers.

▶ Mike Tobin & The Magnettes travel to London to play at the Lambeth Festival.

1962

▶ Formed at The Eagle House Youth Club, The [Bristol] Eagles and vocalist Valerie Mountain perform tracks for the film *Some People,* including 'Johnny's Tune' and 'Bristol Express'.

▶ Russ Conway's final Top 50 hit is 'Always You And Me' which reaches number 33. Conway has had a remarkable 20 chart singles between 1957 and 1962.

▶ Acker Bilk's instrumental 'Stranger on the Shore' is the UK's biggest selling single of 1962: it is in the UK charts for more than 50 weeks, peaking at number two, and is the first Number One single in the United States by a British artist in the era of the modern *Billboard* Hot 100 pop chart.

1963

▶ On August 24, the first edition of *Western Scene* is published. A fortnightly entertainments newspaper, the front cover features Johnny Carr & The Cadillacs with the headline 'The Bristol Sound'.

▶ The Cougars release the single 'Saturday Night At The Duckpond' on EMI Records. An instrumental based on Tchaikovsky's 'Swan Lake' it is banned by the BBC for 'distortion of melody, harmony and rhythm' but nevertheless remains in the charts for eight weeks, peaking at number 33.

▶ The Beatles make their Bristol debut at the Colston Hall on March 15, supporting American stars Tommy Roe and Chris Montez. They then top the bill at the Bath Pavilion on June 10 supported by two local bands – The Colin Anthony Combo and Chet And The Triumphs. The Beatles play the Colston Hall again on November 15.

1964

▶ On Sunday May 10, the Rolling Stones appear at the Colston Hall with several Bristol-based acts supporting including the Echoes, the Avon Cities Jazz & R&B bands and Mike Tobin & The Magnettes.

▶ In August Danny Clarke & The Jaguars play on the steps of Lord Bath's Longleat House at an open air concert to thousands of fans, before the headline act the Rolling Stones appear.

COLSTON HALL - BRISTOL

Entertainments Manager: F. K. Cowley, M.I.M. Ent.

SUNDAY DECEMBER 12TH AT 6.30 P.M.

Brian K. Jones and **Pat Vincent** present

GROUPS GALORE '65

JOHNNY CARR AND THE CADILLACS

BRISTOL's OWN HIT MAKERS

FORCE WEST (Formerly Danny Clarke and The Jaguars)	CHET AND THE TRIUMPHS
THE PENTAGONS	THE SHERRIDANS
DEAN PRINCE AND THE DUKES	
JOHNNY SLADE AND THE VIKINGS	THE ROADRUNNERS
THE FRANKLYN BIG SIX	
THE MEXICANS	THE CONCORDS
THE STRANGE FRUITS	
THE CHEQUERS	THE TEENBEATS
THE DROVERS	THE KYND

Prices: 7/6, 6/-, 5/-, 4/-   All Seats Reserved

Obtainable from Chas. H. Lockier Ltd., 29/31 Queen's Road Bristol (23885

1965

▶ Johnny Carr and The Cadillacs win the *Western Scene* popularity poll for the third year running, voted for by readers of the newspaper.

▶ The Who play at Bristol Corn Exchange on Wednesday December 8. Admission is eight shillings.

▶ Fred Wedlock releases his first record. The 7-inch EP titled 'Volume One' is also the first release on Bristol's Saydisc Specialized Recordings Ltd founded by Gef Lucena. Only 99 copies are pressed to avoid paying purchase tax.

▶ Jazz musicians begin congregating on Sunday mornings at the Old Duke in King Street for informal New Orleans-influenced jam sessions.

1966

▶ In May the New Bristol Centre opens in Frogmore Street. It includes an ice rink, the Heartbeat Discotheque, the Locarno Ballroom, the Mayfair Banqueting Suite, an ABC Cinema and later a casino. It is the largest entertainment complex in Europe.

▶ Roger Cook and Roger Greenaway under the name David and Jonathan reach Number 11 in the charts in January with a cover of the Beatles song 'Michelle'. In July they are in the top ten with the self-penned 'Lovers Of The World Unite'.

▶ Ray Willmott opens the iconic Troubadour folk club in Waterloo Street, Clifton. The first night is Friday, October 7 and the first act is Anderson, Jones, Jackson.

▶ Adge Cutler And The Wurzels release their first single on Columbia Records – 'Drink Up Thy Zider'/'Twice Daily'.

1967

▶ Dave Arbus (violin), Ron Caines (saxophone) and Geoff Nicholson (guitar) form Picture Of Dorian Gray, one of Bristol's first progressive rock bands. They appear in a production of *Two Gentlemen Of Verona* at The Bristol Old Vic then change their name to East Of Eden and move to London, recording two albums for Atlantic Records.

▶ On February 9, Jimi Hendrix is one of the many stars to perform at the Locarno, Frogmore Street.

▶ Terry Brace from Plastic Dog Promotions designs the famous Dug Out club sign.

1968

▶ The Dug Out on Park Row becomes the hub of the underground scene. The Deep Blues Band hold regular sessions and experimental, progressive groups such as Gryptight Thynn, East Of Eden, Obsession, Barnaby Goode and Keith Tippett draw big audiences. Lightshows – First Light, Lightship and Diorama are a crucial element of the events.

▶ In October, the Old Granary, Welsh Back opens. Owned by Dave Bilk, Acker Bilk's brother it is a seven-nights-a-week venue with the emphasis on jazz and blues. On November 15, Chicago blues legend Muddy Waters plays with his full band of American musicians. The Avon Cities Jazz Band support.

▶ The Severn Jazzmen become the first band to play in the downstairs bar at the Old Duke.

1969

▶ With their Monday night sessions at the Dug Out packed to overflowing, Plastic Dog Promotions move their operation to the Old Granary. They begin to book national attractions such as Steamhammer on March 17 and Caravan on May 19.

▶ King Crimson appear at the (Old) Granary on June 30 and Yes play there on July 28.

▶ On the June 3, Frank Zappa And The Mothers Of Invention perform at the Colston Hall. Obviously not a fan of prog rock somebody throws a stink bomb on stage. Famously, Zappa makes the announcement: 'Thank you Bristol. Next time we play here we will have a full programme of Twist numbers – Bristol should be ready for The Twist by then.' After the show Zappa returns to London, but The Mothers plus American roadies are taken to the Granary by the Plastic Dog crew for a drink and to see The Avon Cities Jazz Band. They are then taken to a flat in Clifton and party until dawn.

Adge Cutler And The Wurzels.

▶ Having met at the Dug Out, James Warren of Dawn, Andy Davis and Jim 'Crun' Walter of Gryptight Thynn form a new band called Stackridge Lemon (they later drop the Lemon). Recruiting Billy 'Sparkle' Bent (drums) and Mick 'Mutter' Slater (flute) they are joined later in the year by Mike Evans (violin). They begin to get bookings around the country including at the Marquee in London and support Black Sabbath in Hastings.

▶ On August 24, Slade play the Granary. They are paid £50.

▶ In September, Michael Eavis holds the first Glastonbury Festival at Worthy Farm in Pilton, Somerset. Several Bristol acts appear including Ian A Anderson, and Stackridge. T Rex are the headliners. Admission is £1, including free milk.

▶ On September 18, *Pigsty Hill Light Orchestra Presents* becomes the first album released on the new Village Thing record label based in Clifton.

▶ On November 15, avant garde jazz rock pianist Keith Tippett launches the ambitious *Septober Energy* concert at the Lyceum On The Strand, London. Comprising more then 50 musicians, including members of King Crimson, Soft Machine and Bristol drummer Tony Fennell, they also play at the Colston Hall the following year when the composition is released on a double album produced by Bob Fripp.

1971

▶ On February 1, there is a double bill at the Granary with Balls (fronted by ex-Moody Blues vocalist Denny Laine) and Brewers Droop (who include Dire Straits star Mark Knopfler). The *Bristol Evening Post* refuses to accept an advert for the gig because the combined band names might cause offence.

▶ On February 22, Genesis make their only appearance at the Granary for a fee of £50.

▶ In April, East Of Eden are at number seven in the charts with the instrumental 'Jig A Jig'.

1972

▶ In March Tiffany's (formerly the Glen rock 'n' roll venue), at the top of Blackboy Hill launches a weekly progressive rock night under the title 'Boobs'. The first night features local heroes Stackridge.

▶ BBC TV Bristol broadcast a new music programme featuring mainly local talent called *Stackridge, Squidd and Co*. As well as the two resident bands, guest artists include Wishbone Ash, folk singers Hunt & Turner and Fumble.

▶ David Bowie plays the Anson Rooms supporting Focus at the University Gay Society Annual Ball. It's Bowie's fifth gig as Ziggy Stardust.

1973

▶ Hailing from Sweden, female rock quartet the Ladybirds play at the Granary on March 22. Their main claim to fame is that they perform topless.

▶ Stackridge headline their own nationwide tour with Camel in support. The final date is on home turf on April 1 when they sell out the Bristol Hippodrome.

▶ Bob Marley And The Wailers play the Bamboo Club, St Paul's on May 26.

1974

▶ First Ashton Court free festival. The festival runs on four successive Sundays over the summer. Acts include Fred Wedlock, Pigsty Hill Light Orchestra and Steve Tilston.

▶ The Mael brothers' hit-making band Sparks play at the Victoria Rooms, Clifton promoted by Plastic Dog.

▶ Stackridge release their third album *The Man In The Bowler Hat* on MCA records. Produced by George Martin it is still regarded by critics and fans as one of his greatest works outside of his Beatles canon.

▶ Sunday, May 4. Adge Cutler dies when his MGB sports car hits a patch of grass and crashes into the roundabout at the junction of the Wye Valley Link Road (A466) and the M4.

Adge is returning from a gig at the Crystal Room, Hereford at approximately 4am.

1975

▶ On July 19, Fumble from Weston-super-Mare make one of several appearances at the Granary. Their self-titled album released on Sovereign Records has a classic album sleeve designed by Hipgnosis studios, which catches the eye of David Bowie when browsing a record shop. He is so impressed by their old style rock 'n' roll he invites them to be support band on his American tour. Later their pianist Sean Mayes becomes a member of Bowie's backing group.

1976

▶ Lee Sheriden of Brotherhood Of Man becomes the only Bristolian to date to win the Eurovision Song Contest. Sheriden (real name Roger Pritchard) began his musical career as lead guitarist in Bristol band Dean Prince And The Dukes in the 60s, took up songwriting in the early 70s, changed his name and penned 'Save Your Kisses For Me' which achieved Eurovision glory in March 1976. At the time Sheriden was living in Ashley Down.

▶ In April, after moving labels from MCA to Elton John's Rocket Records, undergoing a change of management and several line-up changes Stackridge make their final appearance at Johnson Hall, Yeovil. They reform briefly in 1999 and again from 2006 to 2015.

🎸 On November 23 the Cortinas play a charity gig in aid of Southmead Hospital's Intensive Care Unit at the Granary. Journalist (and Vice Squad drummer) Shane Baldwin dubs them 'Bristol's most important punk group – no contest.' Guitarist Nick Sheppard later joins the Spics and is in the final line up of the Clash.

🎸 Johnny Britton forms the Primates who are taken under the wing of Clash manager Bernie Rhodes when he spots them supporting Subway Sect at Barton Hill Youth Club, but they've folded by the end of 1977 after moving to London. Other Bristol first-generation punk bands include the Pigs and Social Security.

🎸 Revelation Rockers form.

1977

🎸 Mark Stewart (vocals) and friends John Waddington (guitar) and Simon Underwood (bass) form the Pop Group. They are joined by Gareth Sager (guitar) and Bruce Smith (drums). Dan Catsis replaces Simon Underwood in 1979.

🎸 On January 22, the Cortinas support the Stranglers at the Roxy club in Covent Garden after the band come to Hugh Cornwell's attention following a chance meeting with Nick Sheppard in Bristol. The Cortinas sign to the Step Forward label and release the singles 'Fascist Dictator' in June and 'Defiant Pose' in December.

► Bamboo Club promoter Tony Bullimore brings Jamaican toaster Big Youth to Bristol for two nights at the Exhibition Centre on September 16 and 17.

► Fire breaks out at the Bamboo Club, St Paul's, on the morning on December 18. The club and everything inside (including 15,000 records) is destroyed. The Sex Pistols were due to play there on December 21.

1978

► The Cortinas sign to CBS and release one album, *True Romances*. The band splits by the end of the year.

► The Media including Thomas Brooman on drums, support Siouxsie And The Banshees at Barton Hill Youth Club on January 28.

► John 'The Golden Bowler' and Mauveen Stone take over the Old Duke on June 5 and revive it as a jazz venue. The 'Golden Bowler' refers to the New Orleans Golden Bowler Hat which John would don at the end of an evening and conduct a sing-along of the 'Bog-Enders'.

1979

► *Avon Calling – The Bristol Compilation* is released on Simon Edwards' Heartbeat Records. Artists include Vice Squad, Gl*xo Babies, Europeans, Essential Bop, the Stingrays and the Numbers.

ASHTON COURT FESTIVAL 84

The Bristol Community and WOMAD Festival
Ashton Court Estate
Sat 14th - Sun 15th June 1984
MUSIC   THEATRE   DANCE
KIDS EVENTS : STALLS

▶ The Pop Group release their first album Y on Radar Records. It is produced by dub musician Dennis Bovell.

▶ Black Roots form. Chaos UK form. Vice Squad play their first gig appearing at the Anson Rooms at Bristol University Students' Union on April 12.

1980

▶ The *Bristol Recorder*, a magazine and LP in gatefold sleeve is launched. Bands featured on the first *Recorder* LP are the Electric Guitars, Various Artists, Circus Circus and Joe Public.

▶ Gareth Sager and Bruce Smith form Rip Rig & Panic with singer Neneh Cherry following the demise of the Pop Group. Mark Stewart decamps to London to work on Adrian Sherwood's On-U Sound dub reggae project.

1981

▶ Former Genesis frontman Peter Gabriel appears on three tracks on the second edition of the *Bristol Recorder*. Other artists include Fish Food, the Radicals, X-Certs and the Welders.

▶ Revelation Rockers morph into Talisman and release the single 'Dole Age'.

▶ Although it says 1980 on the label, it was January 1981 that Vice Squad (Beki Bondage, vocals, Dave Bateman, guitar, Mark

Hambly, bass, Shane Baldwin, drums) release 'Last Rockers' on the Riot City label with Simon Edwards of Heartbeat Records. John Peel opens his radio show with 'Last Rockers' every night for a week. The initial pressing of 1,500 sells out in three days and the record goes on to sell 22,000 copies.

► Gerard Langley's band the Blue Aeroplanes first perform under that name at the King Street Art Gallery. They consist of members of the Art Objects plus Nick Jacobs on guitar.

► Former Rodway School (Mangotsfield) pupils Sara Dallin and Keren Woodward move to London together, meet Siobhan Fahey and form Bananarama.

► Ashton Court Festival is banned by Bristol City Council after the 1980 event gets out of control when Hell's Angels take over the site, drugs are on sale and trees set on fire.

► Fred Wedlock's 'Oldest Swinger In Town' peaks at number six in the UK Singles Chart.

► Cheltenham and Bristol funk rock outfit Pigbag release the instrumental classic 'Papa's Got A Brand New Pigbag'.

───────────────── **1982** ─────────────────

► Bananarama sing background vocals on Fun Boy Three's single 'It Ain't What You Do...' which reaches number four in the charts. Terry Hall and Funboy Three return the compliment by backing Bananarama on 'Really Saying Something' which reaches number 5.

▶ The Stonehouse, a folk club and more recently punk venue at the back of the Bunch Of Grapes pub, is demolished to make way for the Spectrum building at the bottom of the M32.

▶ Talisman support the Rolling Stones at Ashton Gate on Sunday, June 27.

▶ The first WOMAD festival is held from Friday 16 to Sunday 18 July at the Royal Bath And West Showground in Shepton Mallet. The festival is founded by Peter Gabriel, Thomas Brooman and the Bristol Recorder team plus Bob Hooton, Mark Kidel, Martin Elbourne and others. Bristol bands Rip Rig & Panic and Black Roots play.

▶ Reggae band Restriction emerge from the Arts Opportunity Theatre project. The original line-up is Rob Smith (guitar) who went on to form Smith & Mighty with Ray Mighty; Karl Williams (vocals) who is Ronnie Size's elder brother; Mark Spence (bass); Andy Clark (drums); Charlie Clarke (saxophone); Basil Anderson (keyboards). The sound engineer is Dave McDonald who went on to work with Portishead. Jendayi Serwah and Eric 'The General' McCarthy replace Karl Williams as lead singer in 1983. 'The General' is Carlton McCarthy's brother who was vocalist with Daddy G on 'Any Love' in 1988, a Massive Attack/Smith & Mighty production.

▶ Heavy metal band Jaguar release their debut single 'Axe Crazy', now regarded as a New Wave Of British Heavy Metal classic.

▶ Pigbag's single 'Papa's Got A Brand New Pigbag', reaches number. 3 in the UK Singles Chart

▶ Grant Marshall, later Daddy G of Massive Attack, becomes resident DJ at the Dug Out, later joined by the Wild Bunch sound system.

––––––––––––––––––– **1983** –––––––––––––––––––

▶ Hip-hop begins to make a major impact of the post-punk Bristol scene with the emergence of collectives such as Wild Bunch, 2 Bad Crew, UD4, Wise Guise and City Rockas. Young graffiti artists such as 3D, Chaos and Crime Inc (FLX, Inkie, Jinx and Nick Walker) produce flyers to publicise underground house parties. The Dug Out club is a hub for this new sound and creativity.

▶ The new *Venue* magazine rock editor Dave Higgitt persuades publisher Dougal Templeton to give Ashton Court Festival free use of the magazine office. So the Festival returns after the ban of 1981 as a one-day event. Bands include Black Roots, Startled Insects, Maximum Joy and Restriction.

▶ Black Roots release eponymous debut album.

▶ Davey Woodward (vocals, guitar), Chris Galvin (bass), Winston Forbes (guitar), Bob Morris (drums) from the Southmead/Lawrence Weston area form the Brilliant Corners. They quickly smooth their rock 'n' roll raw edges to become an indie guitar band and add Dan Pacini on trumpet.

▶ Nick Sheppard joins the Clash to replace Mick Jones.

1984

▶ WOMAD joins forces with Ashton Court Festival for a joint event. WOMAD takes place on the Saturday and Ashton Court on Sunday.

▶ DJs John Stapleton and Ian Dark form Def Con one of the city's most innovative club nights. Stapleton also joins the Blue Aeroplanes who become the first guitar band to have a DJ as part of their set and on studio albums.

1985

▶ Wild Bunch take over Campbell Street at St Paul's Carnival and party till dawn.

▶ New Wave act Red Box (Simon Toulson-Clark and Julian Close) reach number three in the UK Singles Chart with 'Lean On Me (Ah-Li-Ayo)'. It reaches Number One in five countries and is a top five hit in a further 12 countries.

▶ Gary Clail announces his arrival on the Bristol scene with his thunderous dub-reggae sound system. His first single 'Half Cut For Confidence' is released on Adrian Sherwood's On-U-Sound label, also home to Mark Stewart, ex-Pop Group.

--------------------- **1986** ---------------------

▶ The Dug Out club is forced to shut when police object to renewing its licence following complaints by local traders. The Granary also closes.

▶ Bob Dylan visits Bristol to film concert footage at Colston Hall for a film called *Hearts of Fire*.

--------------------- **1987** ---------------------

▶ Jazz saxophonist Andy Sheppard releases his eponymous debut album and begins a career that establishes him as one of Britain's most influential modern jazz artists.

▶ Clare Wadd and Matt Haynes set up Sarah Records in a house in Windmill Hill. Determined to prove you don't have to be based in London to run a successful label, Sarah becomes a leading indie label. Each single features a picture from the city on its centre label. Compilation albums are named after places in and around Bristol and numbered after the buses that go there.

▶ Ex-Cortinas and Clash guitarist Nick Sheppard, Gareth Sager (ex-Pop Group and Rip Rig & Panic guitars and keyboards) are joined by Rich Beale (vocals), Jamie Hill (drums) and Mark

Taylor (bass) to form alternative rock group Head. They release the album *A Snog On The Rocks* on Demon Records.

▶ Western Star Domino Club closes.

1988

▶ Formed as a punk band in 1982, Onslaught are now a heavy metal outfit and sign to London Records in a six-album deal for £1.25 million. Their third album *In Search Of Sanity* is released.

▶ Wild Bunch release *Friends And Countrymen/Look Of Love* EP on 4th And Broadway label. Writing credits are for Milo Johnson, Robert Del Naja and Nellee Hooper. Mushroom is also credited as being part of the Wild Bunch.

▶ First glimpse of Massive Attack with the release of 'Any Love' 12-inch credited to 'Massive Attack featuring Daddy Gee and Carlton'. The record is released on Massive Attack Records (Mass 001). The producers are Massive Attack and Smith & Mighty.

▶ Smith & Mighty release their first two singles, 'Anyone' and 'Walk On' covers of Burt Bacharach and Hal David's 'Anyone Who Had A Heart' and 'Walk On By'. The singer is Jackie Jackson. The records are released on Smith & Mighty's Three Stripe label.

▶ Punky, garage outfit the Seers (Spider, vocals, Leigh

Gary Clail.

Wildman and Kat Day, guitars, Jason Collins, bass, Adrian Blackmore, drums) support the Ramones on a national tour and play a series of dates with Iggy Pop.

▶ Goth rockers Claytown Troupe sign to Island Records and release their *Through The Veil* LP. They are support band for the Cult on the Sonic Temple tour.

▶ Polly Harvey (guitar, saxophone, vocals) joins John Parish, Rob Ellis, Ian Oliver and Jeremy Hogg in percussion-fuelled experimental rock band Automatic Dlamini.

▶ Pirate radio hits Bristol with Emergency Radio, B.A.D, Raw FM and FTP (For The People).

▶ Keyboard player Scott Davidson has a Number One hit with Bros when 'I Owe You Nothing' reaches top spot. Davidson went on to found the *Trade-It* free advertising paper and was Bristol City FC chairman from 1996-2001.

▶ Siobhan Fahey quits Bananarama and forms Shakespears Sister. First Avon Free Festival at Wick.

1989

▶ The Blue Aeroplanes support REM on the UK leg of the *Green* album world tour.

▶ Fresh 4 from Knowle West (Suv, Judge, Flynn and Krust)

and singer Liz E join Bananarama, Russ Conway, Lee Sheriden, East of Eden, Red Box, Fred Wedlock and David and Jonathan by being from Bristol and having a top 10 hit. Their version of the Rose Royce song 'Wishing On A Star' (produced by Smith & Mighty) peaks at number 10 on October 15, 1989.

▶ D J Milo, of Wild Bunch, moves to New York, and later sets up Ruff Disco Records in 1991.

1990

▶ To celebrate his 65th birthday, Russ Conway hosts his first Charity Gala Show to raise money for the Russ Conway Cancer Fund. The event at the Bristol Hippodrome is a sell-out.

▶ Following 1988's Massive Attack/Carlton McCarthy collaboration on *Any Love*, Smith & Mighty produce Carlton McCarthy's album, *The Call Is Strong*.

▶ Poll Tax riots in Bristol.

1991

▶ Polly Harvey, Rob Ellis and Ian Oliver leave Automatic Dlamini to form the PJ Harvey Trio.

▶ Massive Attack (Daddy Gee, Mushroom and 3D from the Wild Bunch) release their debut album *Blue Lines* featuring vocalists Shara Nelson and Horace Andy and rapper Tricky Kid. If you want an exact date for the beginning of what became known as the Bristol Sound, the day *Blue Lines* is released is as good as any – Monday, April 8, 1991.

▶ Geoff Barrow, a tape operator at Bristol's Coach House studio where Massive Attack recorded *Blue Lines*, forms a band with singer Beth Gibbons and jazz guitarist Adrian Utley. Dave McDonald (ex-Restriction) is the sound engineer. The band is named after the Severnside town near Bristol where Barrow grew up – Portishead.

▶ Indie band Strangelove form and play their first gig at Moles club in Bath on October 9.

1992

▶ The Moonflowers play naked at Ashton Court Festival and DJ Paul Oakenfield plays Club YeYo at the Thekla.

▶ Producers and DJs Jody Wisternoff and Nick Warren begin working together pioneering a progressive house music style as Way Out West.

1993

▶ The PJ Harvey Trio splits following a US tour supporting U2. PJ Harvey goes solo.

▶ Artist Felix Braun and Paul Cleaves (FBI Crew) set up Kongcrete Records, releasing house, deep house and techno.

▶ DJ Dazee sets up Ruffneck Ting. "One of the defining points of Bristol's D&B scene," according to *Ethics* magazine in 2006.

1994

▶ Portishead release their debut album *Dummy*. It peaks at number two in the UK Album Chart.

▶ Strangelove's single 'Time For The Rest Of Your Life' is *Q* magazine's Single Of The Year.

▶ Roni Size, DJ Krust and Chris Lewis set up Full Cycle Records, one of the most significant drum and bass labels of the early 90s, issuing releases from Size, Krust, Die, Suv, D Product, Flynn & Flora and more.

1995

▶ Tricky releases his debut album *Maxinquaye* featuring vocalist Martina Topley-Bird. The album is named after Tricky's late mother Maxine Quaye. It sells 100,000 in the first few months of its release and reaches number three in the UK Album Chart.

▶ Portishead win the Mercury Music prize for their album *Dummy*. PJ Harvey (*To Bring You My Love*) and Tricky (*Maxinquaye*) are shortlisted.

▶ John Parish from Automatic Dlamini joins PJ Harvey on her third studio album *To Bring You My Love*. The album goes on to sell one million copies worldwide.

▶ Sarah Records release their final compilation CD, *There And Back Again Lane*, which accompanies a booklet telling the Sarah story. A farewell party is held on the Thekla.

▶ Massive Attack launch their Melankolic label. The first release is *Skylarking* by Horace Andy.

1996

▶ Tricky is the first of the acts now associated with the Bristol Sound to release a second album. *Pre-Millennium Tension* is recorded mainly in Jamaica and New York and displays a harder, darker edge to his work

▶ DJs Flynn & Flora release the *Native Drums* LP – one of the first drum and bass acts to compile tracks and release them as a full album.

▶ Bristol Central Library begins to dispose of its vinyl records.

1997

▶ Roni Size and Reprazent win the Mercury Music Prize for their album *New Forms*.

▶ Jamie Eastman sets up Hombre record label, releasing breaks, beats and hip-hop tracks made by local artists. Banksy designs some of the early record sleeves.

▶ Way Out West peak at number 15 in the UK Singles Chart with 'The Gift'.

___ **1998** ___

▶ Mushroom makes his final appearance with Massive Attack when they play the Anson Rooms, Bristol in November.

▶ Arrival of the Breakbeat Era drum and bass project, consisting of producers Roni Size and DJ Die, with Leonie Laws providing vocals.

___ **1999** ___

▶ In September, Mushroom makes the official announcement that he has left Massive Attack.

▶ Drum and bass duo Darren Decoder and Markee Substance team up with Welsh singer Sian Lewis to form Kosheen.

▶ Sean Cook (vocals, bass) Mike Mooney (guitar) and Damon Reece (drums) form Lupine Howl and record sessions with Massive Attack, but the results are not released.

▶ Krust (Fresh 4) releases his debut album *Coded Language*, a drum and bass groundbreaker featuring American rapper and poet Saul Williams.

▶ Breakbeat Era release the *Ultra Obscence* LP – a pioneering album fusing rock, pop and drum and bass.

DJ Krust.

2000

▶ Russ Conway dies in Eastbourne on November 15 aged 75. He sold 30 million records and had 17 consecutive top 20 hits.

2001

▶ Kosheen release the album *Resist* in September which reaches number eight in the UK Album Chart.

▶ PJ Harvey wins the Mercury Music Prize for her album *Stories From The City, Stories From The Sea*.

▶ Stanton Warriors release their multi-award-winning breakbeat compilation, *The Stanton Sessions*.

2002

▶ Nick Talbot, performing under the name Gravenhurst releases his *Gas Mask Days* EP. His dark and atmospheric sound attracts a cult following.

2003

▶ Kosheen's second album, *Kokopelli* is released in August and reaches number seven in the UK Album Chart.

▶ DJ Krust (Fresh 4) and DJ Die (Reprazent) release the classic drum and bass LP *I Kamanchi* on Full Cycle.

▶ Massive Attack release their long-awaited fourth LP, the first without Mushroom. Daddy G doesn't contribute to the album but remains part of Massive Attack. Despite this, *100th Window* hits Number One in the UK Album Chart. Massive Attack play a one-off show in Queen Square to 20,000 fans.

▶ Geoff Barrow (Portishead) sets up the fiercely experimental and independent Invada Records with Paul Horlick (Fat Paul) from The Croft and later The Exchange. Bands signed to Invada include Gonga, Team Brick, Atavist, Joe Volk, Crippled Black Phoenix and the Heads.

2004

▶ Massive Attack's *Collected* compilation album peaks at number two in the UK Album Chart.

▶ Daddy Gee from Massive Attack releases *DJ Kicks*, a brilliant selection of tracks he plays out as a DJ. It's a rare solo release from the Massive Attack and Wild Bunch founder.

2005

▶ Bristol Reggae Society is founded at Bristol University and is still thriving in 2018 with regular events at Cosies, Trinity and other venues.

2006

▶ Tom Ford (aka Peverelist) of Rooted Records launches the Punch Drunk record label as a showcase for local artists involved with the local dubstep scene.

2007

▶ Dubstep artist Pinch (aka Rob Ellis) releases his first album *Underwater Dancehall* on his own Tectonic label. He quickly becomes one of the most influential on the dubstep scene with a deep and spacious sound and influences as wide as world music and dancehall. Like fellow Bristolians Gary Clail and Mark Stewart, Pinch goes on to work closely with On-U Sounds bass guru Adrian Sherwood.

▶ It's the end of Ashton Court Festival (or Bristol Community Festival at Ashton Court to be precise). After 34 years of struggling against all odds and somehow pulling through, a combination of Bristol City Council and torrential rain eventually bring down the curtain. The Council move the festival to a new (badly drained) site and then it rains making it impossible for emergency vehicles to access the site. The Sunday of the festival is cancelled leaving organisers with huge debts and on Friday July 20, Bristol Community Festival Ltd announce it has begun the winding up process.

2008

▶ Former St Mary Redcliffe and Temple pupil Beth Rowley goes straight into the UK Album Chart at number six with her soul and gospel tinged debut LP *Little Dreamer*.

▶ Folk outfit This Is The Kit (Kate Stables) team up with long-time PJ Harvey producer John Parish to release their first album *Krulle Bol*.

2009

▶ Geoff Barrow of Portishead forms krautrock trio Beak> with Billy Fuller and Matt Williams.

▶ Chris Farrell founds the Idle Hands dance music record label.

▶ Joker (real name Liam McLean) is named King Of Bass in *XLR8R* magazine. The artist and producer began releasing dubstep and grime tunes in 2007 and is recognised as one of the forerunners of the subgenre purple sound distinguished by its off-kilter and broken beats.

▶ Julio Bashmore (Mathew Walker) releases his first record *Julio Bashmore EP* and quickly becomes established as one of the leading producers and DJs on the house music scene. His Broadwalk Records label is named after the Broadwalk shopping centre near his mum's house in Knowle.

2010

▶ Fred Wedlock dies on March 4 aged 67.

▶ The Pop Group reform to play the All Tomorrow's Parties festival curated by *Simpsons* creator Matt Groening.

2011

▶ PJ Harvey wins the Mercury Music Prize for her album *Let England Shake*. She is the first person to win on two occasions.

▶ 'Louder' by Sian Lewis from Kosheen and DJ Fresh is the first dubstep single to reach Number One in the UK Chart.

▶ DJ Die from Reprazent, Full Cycle and Breakbeat Era founds his Gutterfunk label.

▶ George Ezra enrols at BIMM (British & Irish Modern Music institute) in Bristol and within a year has signed to Columbia Records and goes on to become a recording sensation.

▶ Producers Fuzzface (Geoff Barrow of Portishead) 7stu7 (Portishead sound engineer Stuart Matthews) and Katalyst (one of Barrow's partners in the Australian label Invada Records) form hip-hop collective Quakers, a group of 35 hip-hop artists. Their music first appears on Banksy's 2011 film *Exit Through The Gift Shop*.

2012

▶ Producer Rhythmic Theory, Chris Farrell (Idle Hands) and Shanti Celeste found the Brstl record label. Punk rock newcomers Idles release the *Welcome EP*.

▶ House music producer and DJ Julio Bashmore (aka Matt Walker) releases 'Au Seve', described as "a major club smash" by *Time Out*.

▶ Kahn and Neek launch their Bandulu label aimed at promoting underground grime, dubstep and reggae artists.

2013

▶ Grime/hip-hop artist K*ners (real name Horaine Ferguson) releases the single 'Bristol Grammar'.

▶ Young Echo, a loose collective of experimental producers united by a love of bass, release their debut album *Nexus*.

▶ Shanti Celeste releases debut EP, *Need Your Lovin' (Baby)*.

2014

▶ Acker Bilk dies aged 85 on November 2.

▶ Death of DJ Flora.

▶ Celestine Walcott-Gordon reaches the knock-out stage of the BBC talent show *The Voice* and goes on to become the vocalist for Italian house music group Black Box.

2015

▶ DJ Derek is reported missing in July. His remains are found near Cribbs Causeway in March 2016.

▶ The Pop Group release *Citizen Zombie*, their first studio album for 35 years.

▶ Ossia releases the groundbreaking single 'Red-X' a sort of mix of slowed down reggae, electronica and sound effects.

2016

▶ Massive Attack headline the first Downs Festival organised by Team Love. Other acts include Idle Hands, Stryda, Bristol Hifi, Pinch, DJ Krust and Smith & Mighty.

▶ Kosheen officially disband after releasing five albums.

▶ J Morrison releases deep house sensation *Freedom* EP on Alfresco Disco label.

2017

▶ Siobhan Fahey rejoins Bananarama for the *Original Line-Up Tour*. Bananarama have sold an estimated 40 million records.

▶ Way Out West release their fifth studio album, *Tuesday Maybe*, in June. Idles release their first LP *Brutalism*.

2018

▶ Thomas Brooman (Womad founder), Mike Darby (Bristol Archive Records) and Syd Bird release Volume 4 of the *Bristol Recorder* 37 years after Volume 3. Artists include Celestine, LICE, Dr Meaker, Michael Padron, Laid Blak, Patrick Duff, the Shimmer Band, Firewoodisland and Gary Clail Sound System.

▶ St Paul's Carnival celebrates its 50th anniversary.

▶ M Shed exhibition Bristol Music: Seven Decades Of Sound opens in May.

A BIG LIST
OF BRISTOL
ARTISTS

ACKER BILK

Born in Pensford in 1929, Bernard Stanley Bilk was nicknamed 'Acker' which is Somerset slang for 'mate'. He worked at the WD & HO Wills tobacco factory in Bedminster after leaving school and learned clarinet while undertaking National Service in the Suez Canal zone. As a youngster, Bilk lost half a finger in a sledging accident and claimed this affected his distinctive clarinet sound. While touring Germany, his band adopted the bowler hats style. He released the single 'Summer Set' in 1960 (co-written with well-known Bristol jazz pianist Dave Collett) which reached number five in the UK Singles Chart. Four more chart singles followed, but it was the success of 'Stranger On The Shore' released in 1962 that made Acker Bilk an international star.

The melody was originally called 'Jenny' after his daughter but the name was changed when it was chosen as the theme music for the *Stranger On The Shore* BBC drama serial. 'Stranger On The Shore' peaked at number two and spent 55 weeks in the UK Singles Chart. It was Number One in America making Bilk the second British artist to achieve this landmark. Vera Lynn was the first and the Beatles the third.

Acker Bilk died on November 2, 2014 aged 85.

ADGE CUTLER

Alan John Cutler was born in a nursing home in Portishead, Somerset on November 12, 1931 six miles from the family home on Nailsea High Street. As a young man on the Bristol folk and jazz scene centred around the Crown and Dove in Rupert

Street he roadied for Acker Bilk. In 1966 he walked into John Miles' office at 81 Whiteladies Road and persuaded the music impresario to back his idea for a Somerset folk act called Adge Cutler And The Mangold Wurzels – the Mangold got dropped but Miles bought into Adge's plan and legend has it that Adge took his last five pound note to Raselles pawnbroker's in Old Market and spent it on corduroy trousers for the Wurzels' stage costumes.

Early in 1967 his debut single 'Drink Up Thy Zider' sold 50,000 copies and made the lower reaches of the charts. The B-side was the risqué 'Twice Daily' which was banned by the BBC but when the juke box figures came in they showed something like 26,000 plays for 'Drink Up Thy Zider' and 256,000 plays for 'Twice Daily'.

Adge and The Wurzels affectionately captured something essential about the nature of Somerset life and were on the brink of major success with a TV show in their grasp when Adge died. He was travelling back from a gig in Hereford at about 4am on May 4, 1974, when his MGB sports car hit a patch of grass and crashed into the roundabout at the junction of the Wye Valley Link Road (A466) and the M4.

ANDY SHEPPARD

Jazz saxophonist Andy Sheppard only started playing music aged 19 when his life was changed by listening to John Coltrane. Instead of going to art college, Sheppard took up the saxophone and honed his skills in the jazz clubs and bars of the UK and Europe as well as playing in big bands. In 1986 he won a competition and was signed to Island Records subsidiary Antilles. His jazz style is progressive, experimental and distinctive, partly due to him perfecting a circular breathing technique. Sheppard is an internationally acclaimed jazz superstar, but you'll occasionally find him playing some of Bristol's more intimate venues.

BANANARAMA

Former Rodway School (Mangotsfield) pupils Sara Dallin and Keren Woodward moved to London together in 1981, met Siobhan Fahey and formed Bananarama. They sang background vocals on Fun Boy Three's 1982 single 'It Ain't What You Do...' which reached number four in the charts. Terry Hall and Funboy Three returned the compliment by backing Bananarama on 'Really Saying Something' which reached number 5 in the same year. Fahey quit Bananarama in 1988 to form Shakespears Sister. She was replaced by Jacquie O'Sullivan who stayed for three years, but essentially Bananarama were the two Bristolians until 2017 when Fahey rejoined for the *Original Line-Up Tour*. Bananarama have sold 40 million records and between 1982 and 2009 they had 28 singles reach the Top 50 of the UK Singles Chart.

BEAK>

Beak> are Geoff Barrow from Portishead, Billy Fuller and Will Young who replaced original member Matt Williams in 2016. They produce an electronic form of krautrock sometimes recorded live in one room.

BETH ROWLEY

Born in Peru in 1981, Rowley's parents moved back to Bristol when she was two. She formed her first band while still a pupil at St Mary Redcliffe School and went on to study music in Weston-super-Mare and Brighton. Rowley's vocal style covers influences from funk and soul to rock and gospel. Her debut LP *Little Dreamer* went straight into the UK Album Chart at number six.

BLACK ROOTS

Black Roots formed in 1979 and established themselves as one of the leading British reggae acts of the 1980s and early 1990s alongside the likes of Aswad, Steel Pulse and Misty In Roots. The original line-up of the band included Errol Brown (vocals), Delroy O'Gilvie (vocals), Kondwani Ngozi (congas, vocals), Jabulani Ngozi (rhythm guitar), Cordell Francis (lead guitar), Trevor Seivwright (drums), and Derrick King (bass guitar). They folded in the mid 90s but reformed in 2010, performed their first live show in almost 20 years when they played Trinity in Old Market and released new material on Bristol's Sugar Shack Records in 2012. They continue to tour and release material on their Nubian label.

BLUE AEROPLANES

They first performed in 1981 and in 2017 released one of their finest albums, *Welcome, Stranger!* The constant factor in this remarkable history is singer and songwriter Gerard Langley who has fronted scores of musicians who have been part of the

Blue Aeroplanes over four decades. In fact the official count of permanent and supporting members since the release of debut album *Bop Art* in 1984 is 87. The only other permanent member of the Aeroplanes isn't a musician but dancer Wojtek Dmochowski, who is credited on all albums, but took a break from performing live for several years. Gerard's brother John Langley played drums on all but two of the band's albums. The Aeroplanes defy easy categorisation, but try art rock with indie guitars and a bit of folk. Famous for the mass guitar finale at live shows of Tom Verlaine's 'Breaking In My Heart'.

BRILLIANT CORNERS

A bunch of lads from the Southmead and Lawrence Weston estates announced their arrival with the 1983 release of the rockabilly/psychobilly stomper 'She's Got Fever'. The original line-up of Davey Woodward (vocals, guitar), Chris Galvin (bass), Winston Forbes (guitar), Bob Morris (drums) was joined by Dan Pacini on trumpet. And by the time they released their debut album *Growing Up Absurd* in 1985 the Corners had transformed into an indie band in the style of Orange Juice or the Smiths, but with a style and attitude all of their own. Davey Woodward's sometimes wistful lyrical observations and super-cool delivery combined with a rawness from those housing estate roots set the Brilliant Corners apart. Tragically Chris Galvin died in 1998 by which time the Corners had split and he was with Davey in the Experimental Pop Band.

Blue Aeroplanes.

CHAOS UK

Formed in 1979 in the Portishead/North Somerset area, Chaos UK were still touring in 2018. Anarchic, squat-dwelling, hardcore punks, Chaos UK were central to the UK hardcore scene in the 1980s along with fellow Bristolians Disorder and Discharge from Stoke. None of the original members remain in the band, bass player/vocalist Chaos is said to be penning a memoir, and guitarist Gabba who joined in the 80s is the longest-standing member.

CITY ROCKAS

Breakdancers Lui, Dizzy T and Donovan were one of Bristol's original B-boy crews who were to be found at many of the city's hip-hop jams dating back to 1983. When they started DJing they specialised in classic funk.

CLAYTOWN TROUPE

Weston-super-Mare/Bristol goth rockers who were among the flurry of local bands signed to major labels in the late 80s. Frontman Christian Riou and keyboard player Richard Williams founded the band in 1984 and it went through many line-up changes until guitarist Adrian Bennett joined in 1987.

In 1988 they signed to Island Records and released their debut LP *Through The Veil* in 1989. Their second LP, *Out There*, was released on EMI in 1991. A loyal following, sell-out gigs (mainly outside Bristol) and prestigious support slots didn't convert into big record sales and Claytown Troupe split in 1993. The 'Dungeon Demos' that got the band the Island deal were released on limited-edition vinyl by Bristol Archive Records in 2017.

COLONEL KILGORE'S VIETNAMESE FORMATION SURF TEAM

One of Bristol's most unusual musical adventures. The Kilgores had a massive scooter boy and mod revival following in the early 80s but were also a best-kept secret. No information was ever given from the band – even when advertising gigs, their posters just showed a picture of a helmet and sunglasses (no band name), a venue, date and time. Sometimes the Kilgores would drive through town in US Army-style jeeps on the day of the gig. The stage-shows were based on the *Apocaypse Now* film and the band usually announced their arrival on stage with a crescendo of helicopter blades and 'Wagner's Ride Of The Valkyries'. Everyone in the band was called Chuck, the backing singers were the Chuckettes and venue security dressed in US Army Military Police uniform. All that remains is one album (*U.S.M60/1/A*) and a few YouTube videos. The head Chuck went on to form, Superlube And The Engines before performing with his brother as Butch And Randy and finally taking to the stage as a three-piece band, Loud, Ugly And Crap.

CORTINAS

Arguably, this is the band that marks the beginning of the process that resulted in 'The Bristol Sound'. The Cortinas were the most successful of Bristol's first-wave punk bands.

They formed in 1976 with a line-up of Jeremy Valentine (vocals), Dexter Dalwood (bass), Nick Sheppard (guitar), Mike Fewins (guitar), Daniel Swan (drums) and released two singles 'Fascist Dictator'/'Television Families' and 'Defiant Pose'/'Independence' on their own Step Forward label in 1977. The Cortinas formed when Mark Stewart (Pop Group) introduced Sheppard to Cotham Grammar pupils Dalwood, Valentine and Fewins. They were joined by Swan who went to Ashton Park school. In 1978, the Cortinas signed to CBS released one album, *True Romances*, and split by the end of the year.

CRAZY TRAINS

The Crazy Trains were formed in the early 80s by ex St Bede's pupils John McLean (vocals, harmonica) and Paul Grudzinski (guitar) plus Barry Cooper (guitar), Pete Ahluwahlia (drums) and 15-year-old prodigy Jon Chilcott (bass). They were later joined by Mike Crawford on saxophone and guitar. Influenced by the New York Dolls, Chuck Berry, the Faces, Rolling Stones and 60s garage R&B, they exploded on the Bristol scene with an astonishing energy and rock 'n' roll attitude. Former X-Certs firebrand Neil Mackie took over on drums and former Stackridge manager Mike Tobin picked up the band and signed them to new label Spellbound for a reported £250,000. Two singles were released on Spellbound but then the band fell out with the label, who held them to their four year contract, but refused to release more material. Inevitably the Crazy Trains split up.

DAVID AND JONATHAN

One of the most successful songwriting partnerships ever, Roger Cook and Roger Greenaway were born in Bristol in 1940 and 1938 respectively. Cook lived at 8 Forest Road, Fishponds; Greenaway was brought up at 98 Spring Hill, Kingswood. After knocking about with various Bristol bands (such as the Kestrels), they were discovered in 1965 by Beatles producer George Martin. Martin's wife, Judy, suggested they record under the name David and Jonathan and they reached number 11 in the charts with Lennon and McCartney's 'Michelle' in 1966.

A string of other singles followed, but it is as songwriters that Cook and Greenaway made a huge impact. They've written for artists including Gene Pitney ('Something's Gotten Hold Of My Heart'), Cilla Black, Cliff Richard, Kathy Kirby, Hank Marvin, Deep Purple and the Sweet, to name but a few. Cook joined Blue Mink in 1969 and recorded Cook and Greenaway's anti-racism classic 'Melting Pot'.

But it's as the writers of the 1970 Coca-Cola jingle 'I'd Like To Buy The World A Coke', that Cook and Greenaway reached an audience of millions. This was recorded as 'I'd Like To Teach The World To Sing' by the New Seekers and released in December 1971. It brought Cook and Greenaway their first Number One in January 1972. In that month, three of the top four chart songs were Cook and Greenaway creations: at number two was 'Softly Whispering I Love You' (the Congregation) and Cilla was at number four with 'Something Tells Me Something's Gonna Happen Tonight'. They were prevented from a straight top three by the number two sound of Benny Hill with 'Ernie: The Fastest Milkman In The West'.

DEAN PRINCE AND THE DUKES

Dennis Small aka Dean Prince in common with so many teenagers of the time, started out playing guitar and singing during the late Fifties skiffle era. His first group in 1959 was The Monarchs, but in March 1960 they changed their name to Dean Prince And The Dukes with the line up of Dean Prince (vocals), Ronnie Roach (lead guitar), Pete Hayden (bass), Clive Saunders (rhythm guitar) and Johnny Day (drums). In May 1961, Ronnie Roach left the band and was replaced by Roger Pritchard.

In the early 70s, Pritchard changed his name to Lee Sheriden, left the band and embarked on a career as a songwriter. He joined Brotherhood Of Man as a writer/performer, and enjoyed huge success with three Number One singles, including the Eurovision Song Contest winner 'Save Your Kisses For Me' in March 1976.

DJ DEREK

Derek Serpell-Morris was the old bloke in the cardigan in the corner of The Star and Garter playing a cool set of obscure ska. He went on to become a leading figure in the world of dub, reggae and ska. His Trojan collection *DJ Derek Presents Sweet Memory Sounds* was released in the summer of 2006 and he was a regular at many of Europe's leading festivals. He used to be an accountant at Fry's but gave it all up to play ska and reggae. In July 2015 Derek went missing. He was last seen leaving his beloved Wetherspoons on Corn Street and the following day his bus pass was used on the 78 service to Cribbs Causeway, but it is not known if it was used by Derek. His body was found in Patchway, near Cribbs Causeway in March 2016.

DJ DIE

DJ Die is a founder of drum and bass label Full Cycle and a member of Reprazent who won the Mercury Music Prize with Roni Size in 1997 for the album *New Forms*. Die has been at the forefront of the electronic music scene ever since through various projects and partnerships including Breakbeat Era and Gutterfunk.

ENTERPRISE SOUND SYSTEM

Enterprise sound system was one of Bristol's most respected sounds during its operation, 1975-1991. Whether the sound system was basking in the glory of St Paul's Carnival or providing life to a house party, Enterprise was truly appreciated. After a 14-year hiatus, Pappa Roots evolved out of Enterprise and continues to play regular dances in Bristol.

FBI CREW

Operating between 1984-1989, FBI were one of the city's leading hip-hop crews, particularly on the house party scene. Members included Paul Cleaves, Mark Cleaves, Phil Jones, Paul Smart and Dave McCarthy.

FLATMATES

Formed in 1985, the Flatmates were one of the city's leading indie bands. Formed by guitarist Martin Whitehead and Rocker (drums), they were fronted by Debbie Haynes. The original bass player Kath Beach left and was replaced by Sarah Fletcher. It was this line-up that perfected the three-minute, sugar-coated pop melodies that made the Flatmates so popular. 'Happy All The Time' reached number three in the indie charts and 'You're Gonna Cry' peaked at number five in 1987. 'Shimmer' and the 'Janice Long Sessions' both reached number two in 1988 and their final single 'Heaven Knows' was number 10. The Flatmates split up in 1989.

FLYNN & FLORA

Flynn from Fresh 4 and DJ Flora were hugely respected drum and bass producers on the underground scene and released a string of singles mainly on their own Independent Dealers label mainly between 1994 and 2001. Also influential among the city's reggae and jungle DJs. Flora passed away in 2014.

FRANKLYN BIG SIX

Friendly rivals for several years in their respective bands, Mike Tobin (vocals), Al Read (guitar) and Terry Brace (bass), joined together in 1965 to from a new soul outfit the Franklyn Big Six. The line up was completed by Frank Fennell (saxophones), Bob Baker (saxophones) and Frank's brother Tony Fennell on drums. They were then joined by 15-year-old Joanne Justice. Mainly performing the music of artists such as Otis Redding,

James Brown, Ike & Tina Turner, plus some Jazz instrumentals they became very popular amongst the art college students and appeared at the Annual Arts Ball . They also played the Colston Hall and were regulars at the recently opened Mandrake Night Club in Frogmore Street. Frank Fennell was a lecturer at the West of England College of Art at Bower Ashton and with his influence the FB6 decorated their stages with props designed in the pop art style.

FRED WEDLOCK

Fred Wedlock was born in 1942 during the Second World War when most of Bristol's oldest areas were destroyed by bombs. He was brought up in the heart of the city in his parents' pub, the York House, a George's Brewery pub at 16 Phippen Street, Redcliffe. He later claimed that his first public engagement was as a toddler singing to dockers in the bar. He became a star of the vibrant Bristol folk scene of the 60s especially at the dockside Bathurst Hotel and at the Troubadour Club in Clifton.

In the 70s he joined the likes of Billy Connolly, Jasper Carrott and Mike Harding as one of folk's leading comedy entertainers. In 1981 his single 'Oldest Swinger In Town' reached number six in the UK Singles Chart and propelled Wedlock onto the national stage. But Fred was most at home in the West Country. In 1997 he performed in ACH Smith's play *Up The Feeder And Down The Mouth* at Bristol Old Vic. He was also a popular TV presenter, in particular with co-host Sherrie Eugene on HTV's *The Good Neighbour Show*.

Fred Wedlock died on March 4, 2010.

Fresh 4 and Liz E.

FRESH 4 (CHILDREN OF THE GHETTO) AND LIZ E

Straight outta Knowle West, Fresh 4 were brothers Flynn and Krust plus Suv and Judge. Flynn was introduced to producers Rob Smith and Ray Mighty by DJ Flora who liked Fresh 4's idea for reworking the Rose Royce song 'Wishing On A Star' and Liz E (Liz Ellis) was recruited as singer. The story goes that a snatch of the tune was left on an answerphone at Virgin Records and within weeks Fresh 4 and Liz E were signed. 'Wishing On A Star' peaked at number 10 in the UK Singles Chart on October 15, 1989. The follow-up singles 'Release Yourself' and 'Compared To What' weren't as successful and following disagreements with the record company Fresh 4's debut album was never released. In 2015 Bristol Archive Records released *Fresh 4 The Lost Tapes* on limited-edition vinyl.

GARY CLAIL

The apocryphal story about Gary Clail is that the queue to get out of a gig at the Western Star Domino Club was as long as the queue to get in, such was the volume of Clail's bass-heavy dub soundsystem.

A scaffolder and roofer by trade, Clail, from Barton Hill, discovered the delights of the Dug Out and various blues clubs at an early age. He took his love of dub reggae to Adrian Sherwood's On-U Sound collective where his soundsystem supported bands such as African Headcharge. His singles 'Human Nature' and 'Beef' (featuring Bim Sherman) were big club hits and crossed over into the mainstream charts. His most successful album was *The Emotional Hooligan* released in 1991. After almost a decade without releasing new material, Clail returned in 2014 with his *Nail It To The Mast* LP.

GEORGE EZRA

He's not from Bristol, but George Ezra moved to the city in 2011 to study at the city's British and Irish Modern Music Institute (BIMM). Within a year he had signed to Columbia Records and in 2013 his first single 'Budapest' was a hit across the world.

GL*XO BABIES

They came, they produced some brilliant post-punk tunes, they split up and then came back again in an even more experimental form. Seek out the tunes 'This Is Your Life', 'It's Irrational', and 'Who Killed Bruce Lee' if you want to know what the Gl*xo Babies are about.

HAZEL WINTER

A critic once described Hazel Winter's music as 'The sound of a quite unhinging ferocity... a terrific burst of whispery nastiness'. Hard rock guitar and gritty surrealism are the mainstays of Winter's music. She was once in the Blue Aeroplanes and in 2018 released some of her finest work on the *Courtesan* album with her band the Flux Capacitors.

HEAD

Decadent is the word that best describes Head's style of sleazy rock music. Head combined the punk roots of guitarists Nick

Sheppard (Cortinas, Clash) and Gareth Sager (Pop Group, Rip Rig & Panic) with Rich Beales (vocals), Jamie Hill (drums) and Mark Taylor (bass). Despite some serious backing from Virgin Records, Head remained too leftfield to court mainstream success but released three fine albums *A Snog On The Rocks* (Demon 1987), *Tales Of Ordinary Madness* (Virgin, 1988) and *Intoxicator* (Virgin, 1999).

IDLES

Political punk rockers who formed in 2012 and five years later released their debut album *Brutalism* to much critical acclaim. Idles are Joe Talbot (vocals), Mark Bowen (guitar), Adam Devonshire (bass), Lee Kiernan (guitar) and Jon Beavis (drums). *Brutalism* is so called because it marks the same philosophy as the brutalist architecture movement of stripping everything back to fundamental principles. In this case it's an affirmation of hi-energy punk music and sneering at middle class values and aspirations.

JACKIE JACKSON

The voice that helped propel Smith & Mighty to the forefront of 80s underground dance music. Jackie Jackson was the featured vocalist on the first two Smith & Mighty tunes 'Anyone' and 'Walk On' (both released in 1988).

JAGUAR

Heavy metal outfit formed in 1979 with an original line-up of Garry Pepperd (guitar) Jeff Cox (bass, vocals) and Chris Lovell (drums). Jaguar did well across Europe and in Asia as one of the New Wave Of British Heavy Metal bands and in 1982 released the single 'Axe Crazy' now considered a NWOBHM classic.

JAH LOKKO SOUND SYSTEM

Big D, founder of Jah Lokko, is one of Bristol's most illustrious sound system figures. He runs Jah Lokko alongside his two cousins, Lloyd and Snoopy. Jah Lokko was built in 1976 and it continues to be utilised regularly not only as traditional roots sound but also as a vessel for other artists to play on. As one of the founders of Bristol Dub Club, Jah Lokko can be heard regularly at the monthly sound clash events they host at the Black Swan.

JOHN STAPLETON

DJ John Stapleton moved to Bristol in the late 70s and became a regular on the decks at hip-hop parties before getting his own Friday night slot at the Western Star Domino Club and launching the electro/funk Club Foot night at the Tropic Club. But it is as the founder of the Def Con club nights (along with Ian Dark from the Z Boys graffiti crew) that Stapleton made his biggest impact. The Def Con nights at the Thekla were legendary for their progressive mix of acid house, funk and hip-hop. Stapleton also performed with the Blue Aeroplanes and is credited on three albums between 1985-88. A compulsive collector of tunes, he runs Wanted Records in St Nicholas Market and is a regular DJ at several club nights.

JOHNNY CARR AND THE CADILLACS

Johnny Carr and The Cadillacs made their debut at The Railway Club, Temple Meads on December 15, 1959 with the line up of Dave Faye (vocals), Pete O'Connell (lead guitar), Mervyn Alexander (rhythm guitar), Gary Keller (bass) and Dave Purslow (drums). On March 11, 1960 singer Cornelius 'Con' O'Sullivan replaced Dave Faye becoming the new 'Johnny Carr'.

In July and August 1961, they performed at the famous Kaiser Keller club in Hamburg, Germany taking over from a Liverpool band the Silver Beatles (who later dropped Silver from their name and became rather well known). They were one of the most popular bands in Bristol and were well-known for covering the latest American songs as soon as they were released. Johnny Carr And The Cadillacs won the Best Band award in *Western Scene* magazine three years in a row between 1963-65.

JOKER

Liam McLean (aka Joker) is a record producer working mainly in dubstep and grime who is also credited as being the forerunner of the purple sound electronic genre distinguished by its broken beats and synthesizer effects. Best known for his single 'Digidesign' from 2009.

JASHWA MOSES

Joshua Moses (he later changed the spelling of his first name) is a roots reggae singer whose family moved from St

Catherine's in Jamaica to Bristol when he was a teenager. Moses won a competition at the Bamboo Club which resulted in him recording his song 'Africa' with producer Dennis Bovell in a London studio. It was released on the More Cut label and was a top 10 hit in the Black Echo reggae chart. Back in Bristol, Moses was one of the artists involved with founding the Shoc Wave label in 1979 and recorded the track 'Pretty Girl'. Fast Forward to 2012 when Bristol Archive Records released the LP *Joshua To Jashwa 30 Years In The Wilderness* as well as re-issuing 'Pretty Girl' and putting out an unreleased track from 1983 called 'Rise Up'.

JULIO BASHMORE

House music producer with a string of big club hits to his name most notably 'Battle For Middle You' (2011), 'Au Seve' (2012) and 'Peppermint' (2014).

K*NERS

Grime and hip-hop producer who has been on the scene since 2002 and had his biggest success with the outstanding 'Bristol Grammar' in 2013. Real name Horaine Ferguson.

KEITH CHRISTMAS

He's from Essex, but pitched up on the Bristol folk scene in the 1960s when he was a student at the School of Architecture at Bath University. In a non-conventional career, Christmas was booked for the first Glastonbury Festival, played guitar on David Bowie's 'Space Oddity', set up a commune in Vobster in the Mendips, recorded with acid rock outfit Magic Muscle, signed to Emerson Lake and Palmer's Manticore label and was a music teacher at Ashton Park school. His finest work is considered to be the five folk-style albums released between 1969 and 1976 in particular *Stimulus* and *Fable Of The Wings*. In 2016 he released the album *Crazy Dancing Days*.

KEITH TIPPETT

Tippett was born in Southmead and went to Greenway Secondary Modern school where he formed a brass band called the KT Trad Lads when he was 14 in 1961. A few years later he was playing in a modern jazz trio at the Dug Out. He moved to London in 1967, married singer Julie Driscoll ('This Wheel's On Fire'). Tippett is internationally regarded as one of the most experimental and radical jazz musicians of his generation working with musicians around the globe from his 50-piece band Centipede to King Crimson.

KOSHEEN

Drum and bass trio formed in 2001 by Markee Substance, Darren Decoder and Welsh singer Sian Evans who emerged from the scene around the Ruffneck Ting raves and Breakbeat Culture shop and label. Split in 2016 after releasing five albums, the first two of which made the UK Album Chart Top 10 (*Resist*, number eight and *Kopokelli* number seven). The singles 'Hide You' (2001) and 'All In My Head' (2003) both made the Top 10.

KRUST

After the demise of Fresh 4, DJ Krust and Suv teamed up with Roni Size, DJ Die, Onallee (vocals), Clive Deamer (drums), Si John (electric and upright bass) in Reprazent and was part of the collective that won the 1997 Mercury Music Prize for the album *New Forms*. He continued the drum and bass theme with the ground-breaking *Coded Language* LP featuring Saul Williams on Island Records in 1999, teamed up with DJ Die for *I Kamanchi* on Full Cycle in 2003 and *Hidden Knowledge* (Full Cycle) in 2006.

LAID BLAK

Laid Blak were formed by two veterans of the rave scene DJ Bungy and MC Joe Peng. Bass player Lui traces his roots back to body popping with the City Rockas hip-hop crew from the 80s while Flex (vocals), Stacy (drums), Tim (guitar), Sam (keyboards) and Tita (vocals) complete the line-up. Their music has been described as 'street soul meets reggae'. In 2007, they released the single 'Red' on Brown Punk, a label set up by Tricky and Island Records boss Chris Backwell. The album *About Time* was released on Bristol's Sugar Shack Records in April 2018.

LIONPULSE SOUND SYSTEM

Lionpulse emerged in early 2009 as two friends with a passion for roots, rub a dub and dancehall music. Gerard and Henry devoted years to collecting records before they decided to build the sound system which was launched in 2013. Lionpulse are associated with a new wave of sound system culture, their impact on the Bristol scene continues to be both influential and inspiring for the next generation.

MASSIVE ATTACK

Grant Marshall, Andrew Vowles and Robert Del Naja changed Bristol music for ever. Without the influence of the three core members of the Massive Attack project it's unlikely that Tricky and Portishead would have emerged; there would be no such thing as the Bristol Sound or trip-hop. In fact, there's a strong case for saying that Massive Attack changed music everywhere, such was the towering originality of their debut album *Blue Lines* released in 1991.

To begin to understand where *Blue Lines* came from we need to step back into the undergound world of the Dug Out club and the New York-inspired hip-hop house parties of the 80s where we'd find one of Bristol's earliest hip-hop crews, Wild Bunch. And to understand where Wild Bunch came from we need to go back through the miner's strike and the Battle of the Beanfield to the beginnings of Thatcher's Britain to the earliest days of punk and the crossover with dub reggae.

Bristol kids looking for a new anti-authority as punk faded embraced hip-hop like no other UK city. Wild Bunch (a core of Del Naja, Johnson, Marshall, Hooper and Claude 'Willy Wee' Williams) were a formidable crew with body poppers and crucially the city's first graffiti artist in '3D' Del Naja.

Wild Bunch split following a stressful tour to Japan, there was friction between the various parties but then Andrew

'Mushroom' Vowles joined Grant 'Daddy G' Marshall and Robert '3D' Del Naja bringing with him a curious blend of influences from Pink Floyd and the Mahavishnu Orchestra to Steeleye Span and hip-hop.

Neneh Cherry from post-Pop Group adventurers Rip Rig & Panic and husband producer Cameron McVey took the fledgling Massive Attack under their wings and much of *Blue Lines* was conceived in the spare room of their London home. Nobody anticipated the complete change of direction from the sparse beats of Wild Bunch to the richness and depth of Massive Attack. There were hints of a slower, more soulful treatment from earlier collaborations with Carlton and Smith & Mighty, but when Massive Attack, Shara Nelson, Horace Andy and Tricky Kid unveiled *Blue Lines* the sound was fresh and like nothing that had preceded it.

Four more studio albums and many collaborations have followed, each one a new beginning and a new sound. Since they formed there was friction between the three core members and in 1998/1999 Mushroom left unhappy with the move away from hip-hop and a DJ-driven stage show to a more guitar influenced sound. It's said that Del Naja and Marshall have barely spoken to Mushroom since.

Massive Attack is a collaboration of artists many of them from Bristol, but one of the most important things that Massive Attack have done for the city is to stay in the city. Their influences are worldwide, but somewhere at the core is a Bristol beat.

MAXIMUM JOY

Formed in 1981 by ex-Gl*xo Babies Tony Wrafter (saxophone, trumpet, flute), and Charlie Llewellin (drums) plus Dan Catsis (bass) and John Waddington (guitar) from the Pop Group, Maximum Joy were fronted by livewire vocalist Janine Rainforth. The sound is influenced by punk, funk, reggae and jazz with production by reggae agitators Dennis Bovell and Adrian Sherwood. They produced an album (featuring a brief appearance by Nellee Hooper on percussion and backing vocals) and several singles but Maximum Joy split in 1983. Rainforth re-formed the band in 2015 and in 2017 Idle Hands and Blackest Ever Black released a vinyl compilation of the band's singles *I Can't Stand It Here On A Quiet Night* on the new Silent Street Records label.

MIKE CRAWFORD

He's been close to many of the interesting things that have happened in Bristol since 1979 when he fronted soul covers band the Spics, whose original line up included Nick Sheppard and Johnny Britton on guitar, Thomas Brooman (drums), John Carley (percussion), Rachel Morgan (bass) and backing singers Wendy and Sarah Partridge, Phoebe Beedell, Heidi Hutton and Jo Swan. Crawford has been behind many solo, studio and band collaborations including the Nitecaps, Apache Dropout and most recently Mike Crawford & The Various Sorrows, who also go out as John E Vistic's backing band. He is also stage manager for Portishead.

MOONFLOWERS

Hippies. The Legendary Moonflowers took nothing seriously apart from friendship, drugs, partying and music. Their often magic mushroom-fuelled frolics were fun, naive and the music was great. Because underlying that seemingly chaotic anarcho, acid, funky rock there were some very good musicians. Fronted by the Revd Sonik Ray (Sean O'Neill), the Moonflowers included 'Jesse' Vernon (guitar), Sam Burns (keyboards, saxophone, vocals) Yoddom (Adam Pope on drums), Paul Waterworth (bass), DJ Elmo and later Gina Griffin (vocals) and drummer Toby Pascoe who passed away in 2001.

The Moonflowers formed their own Pop God label, probably because the major labels wouldn't know what to do with them, and released several EPs, singles and LPs between 1987 and 1997, most notably *We Dig Your Earth*, *Get Higher*, *Hash Smits* and *Warshag*. Several other Bristol bands released records on Pop God including Me and Praise Space Electric. In true hippy fashion, the Moonflowers eloped to set up a commune in France and gradually drifted back when the wine ran out.

ONSLAUGHT

Onslaught were formed in 1982 as a hardcore punk band on the Kingswood side of town by guitarist Nige Rockett and drummer Steve Grice. They moved in a thrash metal direction and underwent several line-up changes along the way, gaining a loyal following, especially in Europe. The albums *Power From Hell* (1985) and *The Force* (1986) reinforced the demonic fashion in thrash metal in the 80s. Si Keeler joined as vocalist and in 1988 Onslaught signed to London Records for a reported advance of £1.25 million, but still found time to play their regular Christmas gig at the Lamb pub, on Banjo Island in Cadbury Heath.

Keeler fell out with London and was replaced by Steve Grimmett. Their third album *In Search Of Sanity* (1989) was re-recorded with Grimmett's vocals replacing Keeler's. Despite being an outstanding heavy metal album, the hardcore Onslaught fans rebelled against the sacking of Keeler and a perceived move away from the band's uncompromising thrash metal principles. A home-town show at the Hippodrome was disrupted by a large number of fans chanting 'We want Si'.

Inevitably, Onslaught split. In 2005, Rockett, Grice, Keeler and former bass player James Hinder reformed Onslaught and they found immediate success on the global metal festival circuit. Indeed, in 2017 they claimed to be the first thrash metal band to play Lebanon. It will be no surprise that there have been many line-up changes since 2005 but at the last count, Rockett and Keeler were still at the heart of the band.

OSSIA

Ossia is one of the Young Echo collective of musicians and producers responsible for some of the most experimental dance sounds in Bristol. His 'Red X' single is a mix of slowed down reggae, electronica and crashing sound effects inspired by the personal taped diaries of Wailers founder and guitarist Pete Tosh.

PEVERELIST

Peverelist is a reference to Hatfield Peverel Junglist Massive, Hatfield Peverell being the town of 5,500 people in the middle of Essex where Tom Ford grew up and jungle music a particular early influence. Ford moved to Bristol when he was 18 and became manager of Rooted Records on Gloucester Road which became a centre for the the city's dubstep community. He went on to form the influential Punch Drunk label in 2006 to showcase dubstep artists and other forms of electonica and dance music. One of Ford's best-known tracks is 'Roll With The Punches' from 2007 and in 2017 he released his third album *Tessellations*.

PIGBAG

Although they were formed in Cheltenham in 1980 and had roots in Birmingham it was when they recruited ex-Pop Group bass player Simon Underwood and saxophonist Ollie Moore from Bristol that Pigbag really took shape. Underwood's connections with Dick O'Dell, manager of the Slits and head of Y Records (home of the Pop Group), helped Pigbag land their first gig – supporting the Slits at Romeo And Juliet's in Bristol on October 21, 1980. It was around this time that the fledgling band took the name Pigbag, a reference to founder member Chris Hamlin's cloth bag bearing a screen print of a warthog.

In 1981 Pigbag recorded the track that made their name and continues to be played across the world. 'Papa's Got A Brand New Pigbag' was released in May 1981 and reached number two in the indie charts but didn't make an impact on the mainstream charts. When it was re-issued in March 1982 it reached Number One in the indie charts and number three in the UK Singles Chart. Pigbag split up in 1983.

PINCH

Dubstep artist Pinch (aka Rob Ellis) released his first album *Underwater Dancehall* in 2007 on his own Tectonic label and established himself as one of the most influential artists on the dubstep scene. His trademark deep and spacious style references a wide range of genres from world music and dancehall. Like fellow Bristolians Gary Clail and Mark Stewart, Pinch went on to work closely with On-U Sounds bass guru Adrian Sherwood.

PJ HARVEY AND JOHN PARISH

Polly Jean Harvey first performed with John Parish in a band called Automatic Dlamini in 1988 contributing backing vocals, slide guitar and saxophone. Automatic Dlamini founded by Parish and Rob Ellis were avant garde adventurers driven by percussion, drums, guitar and vocals. They hailed from the Yeovil area, not far from Harvey's Bridport home, but made Bristol their base.

A few years later, Polly took centre stage and in 1991 formed the PJ Harvey Trio with Rob Ellis (drums) and one-time Automatic Dlamini bass player Ian Oliver. The albums *Dry* and *Rid Of Me* and singles including 'Sheela-Na-Gig' were critically acclaimed and commercially successful but in 1993 the PJ Harvey Trio disbanded, Polly went solo and teamed up again with John Parish to record her third studio album *To Bring You My Love*. She has been working with Parish as producer and part of her band ever since.

In 2001, the album *Stories From The City, Stories From The Sea* won the Mercury Music Prize and PJ Harvey repeated that feat in 2011 with *Let England Shake* thus becoming the only artist to win the best album accolade twice.

POP GROUP

Formed in 1977, the Pop Group split up in 1981, but during those few years they made a massive impact on Bristol music and indeed sent shockwaves across the world. They reformed in 2010 and have toured extensively and released new material since. Here is what music journalist Gil Gillespie says of the Pop Group in the *Naked Guide To Bristol* (Tangent Books)...

When Nick Cave and his growling Birthday Party entourage first landed on these shores in 1980, they spent every night going to gigs all over the capital but were shocked and disappointed by the limp, bloodless bands they found. Then one night he saw the Pop Group. The experience changed his life. As part of Channel 4's *Music of the Millennium* series, Cave chose 'We Are All Prostitutes' as his favourite piece of music of all time. 'The beginning of the record is the greatest start of any record, ever,' claims the awesome Aussie. And you wouldn't want to disagree with him.

This is why it's the Pop Group who are cited as being one of the biggest influences on what became known as the Bristol Sound. Even if it's not all that easy to see why, or how, they

Mark Stewart and Gareth Sager (guitar) of the Pop Group.

laid the foundations for Massive Attack. The Pop Group, y'see, made a fearsome, chaotic noise that was always experimental and sometimes plain unlistenable. Their first single, 'She Is Beyond Good And Evil', might have been as infectious as it was deeply disturbing, but much of the *Y* album sounded like a load of out-of-time clanging and primeval hollering, interrupted by the occasional blast of raucous feedback. These elements burned on a fire already white hot with punk, funk and thunderous dub to make a protest music completely out on its own.

So what does all this have to do with the birth of the Wild Bunch and everything that followed them? Crucially, Mark Stewart's unholy Pop Group crew were the first to assimilate the city's black, or more accurately rastafarian, counter-culture into their social life, their worldview, and ultimately their sound. 'With the roots worldview... the feeling of spiritual uplift was undeniable,' says singer Stewart of his dub days. As if this wasn't significant enough, the band also spent their youth going to clubs and listening to dance beats. 'We were like the Bristol funk army,' recalls Stewart. 'We'd go to clubs and dance to records by T-Connection, BT Express, Fatback Band, all this heavy bassline funk.'

And this is how the Pop Group invented the politics of dancing. Their dance was a warped, out-of-shape boogie, but a boogie none the less. 'They even used to dance in the most peculiar way,' remembers one fan. Sadly, by the time they'd made their third album, titled *For How Much Longer Do We Tolerate Mass Murder?*, all the incendiary radicalism had got a bit out of control. Maybe it's best to let the band explain their style of music. 'We were creating a wall of noise for the lyrics to fight against,' sighs bass player Dan Catsis. 'We were challenging the production process, disrespecting the machines.'

Something inevitably had to give, and the members went their separate ways. Gareth Sager formed Rip Rig & Panic, bassist Simon Underwood sought relief in the happy honking of jazz-funkers Pigbag and had a top 10 hit, and Mark Stewart sank still deeper into the well of nihilistic creativity in which he had always prospered.

PORTISHEAD

If you wanted proof that Bristol does things differently, Portishead added to the growing body of evidence with the launch in 1994 of their stunning debut album *Dummy*.

Fusing hip-hop beats, scratching, jazz and blues influences in layers of slow-tempo cool and foreboding, Portishead created a sound that *Melody Maker* described as 'Musique noire for a movie not yet made'.

Portishead were formed by instrumentalist and DJ Geoff Barrow and singer Beth Gibbons in 1991. Barrow was a tape operator at the Coach House studio in Clifton when Massive Attack recorded Blue Lines and the band gave him some studio time to develop his own ideas. He met singer Beth Gibbons who had moved to Bristol from Devon and along with jazz guitarist Adrian Utley and sound engineer Dave McDonald formed the Portishead project. *Dummy* was released on August 22, 1994 and produced three singles 'Numb', 'Sour Times' and 'Glory Box' and won the Mercury Music Prize in 1995.

The second album *Portishead* was released in 1997 signifying a harder edged sound but still distinguished by the soundscapes and beats that underpin the band's style. It took more than a decade for Portishead to release their next studio album, *Third*, which came out in April 2008.

All three band members have worked on a variety of solo projects and collaborations in the intervening years. In 2016 they released a haunting version of ABBA's 'SOS' as a tribute to murdered Labour MP Jo Cox.

QUALITEX SOUND SYSTEM

Qualitex sound system was founded in 1986 by Faada Sojie, Mellow and Jimmy Swing and later joined by Kutty, Ras Baga, Skater B and Didi Skrew. With roots from the town of Yallahs in St Thomas, Jamaica, Qualitex are renowned not only for their exclusive selection but also their custom-built equipment. Crew member Kutty launched his own speaker box building business QSS, in 2010 and builds boxes for both local and international clientele.

QUEEN BEE

Roz Scordilis began her career as DJ Queen Bee in the late 80s on the pirate radio stations Emergency Radio and Respec FM before becoming music programmer for FEM FM, Britain's first all female radio station in 1992. Versatile and energetic, her sets are ever changing and range from ragga to roots to hip-hop to house. Plenty of bootys and mash ups are thrown in, making her a popular attraction on Bristol's club scene and the festival circuit. Queen Bee was Resident DJ on the Jazz World stage at Glastonbury Festival for 10 years, performed at many international WOMAD festivals, and joined up with Daddy G from Massive Attack for performances all over Europe.

In 2007 Mr Benn joined the duo and Bristol HiFi was born. Queen Bee successfully managed Cosies bar in Portland Square, a much-loved Bristol institution. Her knowledge and contacts pulled in many-respected local DJs and a fantastically mixed crowd of discerning music lovers, which attracted comparisons of it being the new Dug Out. Never too serious, never too cheesy, Queen Bee's party style sets and eclectic tastes continue to rock many a dance floor both at home and abroad.

RESTRICTION

Reggae band Restriction emerged from the Arts Opportunity Theatre project in St Paul's and although they were relatively short lived and only released one single, 'Action', their impact was lasting. The original line-up was Rob Smith (guitar) who went on to form Smith & Mighty with Ray Mighty; Karl Williams (vocals) who is Ronnie Size's elder brother; Mark Spence (bass); Andy Clark (drums); Charlie Clarke (saxophone); Basil Anderson (keyboards). The sound engineer was Dave McDonald who went on to work with Portishead. Jendayi Serwah and Eric 'The General' McCarthy replaced Karl

Williams as lead singer in 1983. 'The General' is Carlton McCarthy's brother who was vocalist with Daddy G on 'Any Love' in 1988, a Massive Attack/Smith & Mighty production.

RIP RIG & PANIC

Guitarist Gareth Sager, drummer Bruce Smith plus occasional keyboard player Mark Springer formed Rip Rig & Panic when they left the Pop Group in 1980. They recruited Neneh Cherry as singer and Sean Oliver on bass to form the core of the band. They took their name from a 1965 jazz album by Roland Kirk. By the time of their demise, the Pop Group had pushed their heavy, funk reggae, noise experiment to the brink but Rip Rig & Panic were innovative in a different way, choosing to tread a more free jazz, funk and sometimes surreal path. The results were sometimes patchy, but always interesting.

RITA LYNCH

Rita first appeared on the Bristol scene in the early 80s with an all-woman punk combo called Rita And The Piss Artists, she moved into electronica with God Bless You but since the 90s she's reverted to rock as either a solo artist or fronting a band – often just guitar and drums. She was allegedly taught to play guitar by nuns while at a Catholic school. The power of her playing and vocals can be breathtaking. Rita's debut album *Call Me Your Girlfriend* in 1991 perfectly captured the tenderness and ferocity that distinguishes her work. She performed with the Blue Aeroplanes between 2010-2011.

Neneh Cherry of Rip Rig & Panic.

RONI SIZE/REPRAZENT

When this drum and bass collective won the Mercury Music Prize in 1997 for their debut album *New Forms* they saw off competition from, among others, Radiohead (*The Bends*), Prodigy (*Fat Of The Land*), Suede (*Coming Up*) and the Spice Girls (*Spice*). That's a measure of just how groundbreaking *New Forms* was.

The original Reprazent line-up included Roni Size (programming/keyboards), Onallee (vocals), Si John (electric and upright bass), DJ Die, Suv, Krust (programming production), Clive Deamer (drums), Rob Merrill (guitar), Dynamite MC (raps).

A second album, *In The Mode*, was released in 2000 following which the various members of Reprazent began working on solo projects and collaborations. Roni Size resurrected Reprazent in 2008 and played various festivals. A 20th anniversary remastered, deluxe box set of *New Forms* was released in November 2017.

RUSS CONWAY

Pianist Trevor Herbert Stanford sold an estimated 30 million records over the course of his career as Russ Conway. The boy from Dean Lane, Bedminster had 17 consecutive top-20 hits, his own television shows, mansions, Bentleys and Rolls-Royces. He had no formal musical training and left school agd 14 to work in a solicitors' office. However, he was sent to borstal for three years for theft and taught himself piano while incarcerated. After his release, he entered a Merchant

Navy Training School and, in 1942, joined the Royal Navy. He was awarded the DSM for "gallantry and devotion to duty" in mine-sweeping in the Mediterranean. After four years in the Royal Navy, his long-running stomach ulcer saw him invalided out. He then took a series of dead-end jobs as a salesman, plumber's mate and barman.

Then he stood in for a holidaying club pianist and continued playing in pubs and clubs, and was seen by the choreographer Irving Davies, who was so impressed that he asked him to play piano for stars at rehearsals. He worked for Dennis Lotis, Dorothy Squires and Gracie Fields.

But it was when Conway made it to the BBC's *Billy Cotton Band Show* in the late 1950s that his career took off. Cotton persuaded him to loosen up his playing, and helped create the disciplined freedom of the mature Conway style. His big break came by accident. A musical he had written for the comedian Frankie Howerd, *Mr Venus*, was a write-off, but it led him to writing the score for a TV musical, *Beauty And The Beast*. He had to write a last-minute tune for one brief scene and sitting in the rehearsal room, Conway wrote 16 bars and scribbled 'Side Saddle' beside it in the margin. 'Side Saddle' reached Number One in the UK Singles Chart in 1959 and became Conway's signature tune.

In 1960, when he had his first television show, *Russ Conway And A Few Friends*, he was reputed to be earning £500 a week and moved from a basement flat in Maida Vale, where he personally answered his fan mail, to a mansion, where three full-timers did the job.

Conway smoked 80 cigarettes a day and suffered from nerves and anxiety. The stomach ulcer returned and in 1963, he had a nervous breakdown and then fell and fractured a hip, leaving him paralysed for three days; two years later, at only 38, he had the first of his strokes. By 1971, he had started drinking at a pace which reduced him to near bankruptcy. But his friends helped to pull him through and Conway's career resumed, though on a smaller scale.

At 65, Conway discovered he had cancer. He died in Eastbourne aged 75 on November 15, 2000 just two weeks after his final public performance. Almost 1000 people attended his funeral service at St Mary Redcliffe church on December 6, 2000. Sir Elton John sent flowers and a card that said 'Thanks for being such an inspiration to me, Love Elton'.

SEERS

Their style was like a meeting between the Monkees and the Ramones – 60s garage rock fused with psychedelia, underpinned by punk. The Seers deserved a similar level of success as their contemporaries such as the Stone Roses, Happy Mondays and Wonder Stuff, but this was Bristol pre-Massive Attack when many acts didn't get the recognition they deserved. Formed in 1984, the Seers were Adrian 'Age' Blackmore (drums), Spider (vocals), Leigh Wildman (guitar), Kat Day (guitar) and Jason Collins (bass). A series of misfortunes meant they never got a major deal and the band folded in 1991 leaving us with two albums (*Psych Out* and *Peace Crazies*), a handful of singles and memories of a great live band.

SHANTI CELESTE

Celeste was born in Chile but moved to the United Kingdom when she was 12 with her mother who married an English man. She had her first contact with electronic music at rave parties in the Lake District when she was a teenager. Celeste moved to Bristol for an illustration course at the University of the West of England and met Chris Farrell, a Bristol-based DJ and head of the label Idle Hands. Celeste and Farrell launched the label BRSTL together, on which label Celeste also released her debut single *Need Your Lovin' (Baby)* in 2013. During her time in Bristol, she also set up her own club night called Housework. Celeste was nominated Best Newcomer DJ in the 2015 DJ Awards. In 2016, Celeste relocated to Berlin.

SMITH & MIGHTY

They may not have the profile of Massive Attack, Portishead and Tricky but in terms of influence Rob Smith and Ray Mighty are their equal. Both are products of the punk generation and the fusion with reggae and hip-hop that is one of the defining qualities of the Bristol Sound. Rob Smith was guitarist in reggae band Restriction in the early 80s and when Restriction folded he joined a funk outfit called Sweat where he met Ray Mighty. By 1987 they had set up together as Smith & Mighty. In 1988 they released their first two singles on their Three Stripe label – *Walk On* and *Anyone*, reworkings of Bacharach and David's songs *Walk On By* and *Anyone Who Had A Heart* both featuring singer Jackie Jackson.

The slow beats, stripped back drums and bass-heavy

The Seers.

treatment plus the dreamy vocals created a distinct sound full of warmth and depth. Also in 1988, Smith & Mighty were credited with production for the 'Any Love' single by Massive Attack featuring Daddy Gee and Carlton. In 1989 they produced Fresh 4's cover of the Rose Royce tune *Wishing On A Star* which made number 10 in the UK Singes Chart. In 1990 they produced Carlton McCarthy's album *The Call Is Strong* which in many ways is the 'missing link' between the Bristol hip-hop scene and the 'trip-hop' sound of Massive Attack, Portishead and Tricky.

Smith & Mighty signed a five-year deal with a subsidiary of London Records and that's where it all started to go wrong. The label didn't like the direction of the *Bass Is Maternal* album and when Smith & Mighty refused to compromise they had to see out their deal without any material being released.

Once free of the deal, they worked together on their More Rockers dub project, Alice Perera joined Smith & Mighty as vocalist, Peter D Rose became a regular member of the crew and Tammy Payne was guest vocalist. Rob Smith went on to release the outstanding solo album *Up On The Downs* in 2003 and to record as RSD (Rob Smith Dub). Smith & Mighty still regularly DJ together.

STACKRIDGE

Having met at The Dug Out club in 1969 where their respective bands Dawn and Griptight Thynne often played, guitarists Andy Davis, James Warren and Jim 'Crun' Walter decided to pool their resources in a new group called Stackridge Lemon.

Recruiting recent arrival from Yeovil Mick 'Mutter' Slater on flute and Billy 'Sparkle' Bent on drums and dropping the Lemon from their name they made their debut at a Christmas party at The Old Granary in December 1969.

Signed to management by Mike Tobin, they were soon gaining bookings all over the country and in particular in London. Adding folk musician Mike Evans on violin they became popular for their combination of a madcap eccentric stage show and their broad spectrum of music with influences ranging from the Beatles, Beach Boys and Fairport Convention to Frank Zappa and The Mothers Of Invention. Invited by Mike Tobin to see the band on their home territory at the Victoria Rooms, David Howells of MCA Records offered them a contract and they were soon in the studios recording their first, self-titled album.

Their second Album entitled *Friendliness* was heavily promoted and although it failed to chart they did come fourth in the Brightest Hope section of *Melody Maker*'s Readers' Poll of 1973, above Genesis and Paul McCartney's Wings. They headlined their own nationwide tour with Camel as support band which culminated in a sold out Bristol Hippodrome.

Mike Tobin persuaded George Martin to produce the third Stackridge album *The Man In The Bowler Hat*, which is still regarded as one of Martin's finest achievements outside his Beatles canon. The band released two more albums before breaking up with a final gig in Yeovil in April 1976.

In 1979 Andy Davis and James Warren formed a duo the Korgis with the intention of writing and recording more pop orientated, commercial music. They had two big selling singles 'If I Had You' and 'Everybodys Got To Learn Sometime', the latter song being covered over 20 times by numerous artists including Beck and Zuchero. With three original members, James Warren, Jim Walter and Mike Evans plus new musicians Stackridge reformed briefly in 1999 for three years. Then without Mike Evans, but with founder members Andy Davis and 'Mutter' Slater back on board they got together again in 2006 and continued to perform and record another album *A Victory For Common Sense* on Helium Records, which was produced by Tears For Fears producer Chris Hughes. Finally deciding to retire, the band did one last tour between September and December 2015, which included appearances in Tokyo and a triumphant, emotional final bow at Fiddlers, Bedminster on December 19.

STANTON WARRIORS

Mike Yardley and Dominic Butler have been two of the most in-demand DJs and producers since the release of their award-winning *Stanton Sessions* LP in 2001. Some 15 years later their *Sound Of Punks* LP was as fresh as ever. Stanton Warriors are named after the manhole cover manufacturer and is not a reference to Stanton Drew village near Bristol.

STARTLED INSECTS

Now known as the Insects, these behind-the-scenes maestros have been responsible for many TV and film scores and amassed writing and production credits for some of the biggest names in the business including Massive Attack, Madonna, Goldfrapp and Alison Moyet. Startled Insects formed around 1983 as a collective of three producers and multi-instrumentalists Bob Locke, Tim Norfolk and Richard Grassby-Lewis. They've successfully avoided all publicity but still signed to Island Records and achieved cult status with their 1987 album *Curse Of The Pheremones*. Most recently the Insects and Adrian Utley from Portishead produced the soundtrack for the 2017 film *Becoming Cary Grant*.

STRANGELOVE

If the path of excess does indeed lead to the palace of enlightenment then Strangelove were some seriously enlightened gentlemen. They formed in 1991 after Levitation drummer Dave Francolini spotted Patrick Duff busking. Allegedly Francolini said: 'Get in the car, you're going to be a pop star'. Francolini then recruited guitarist Alex Lee (Blue Aeroplanes) and bass player Joe Allen (who both played with Francolini in a band called the Coltraines when they were pupils at Bristol Grammar School) plus guitarist Julian Pransky Poole (from the Jazz Butcher). Francolini stepped down as drummer after just two gigs and was replaced by John Langley from the Blue Aeroplanes.

And so the adventure began. Duff's tales of despair and sorrow struck a chord, and his impressive, emotionally charged vocals backed by a truly talented bunch of musicians, brought Strangelove to the attention the major labels and they signed to EMI's Food Records.

Tours and support slots with Radiohead, Suede and the Manic Street Preachers plus three stand-out albums brought Strangelove to the brink of greatness, but the drink and drugs took their toll particularly for singer Patrick Duff and Strangelove split up in 1998.

TALISMAN

Originally formed in 1977 as Revelation Rockers, the band changed their name in the early 80s to avoid confusion with a band from London called Revelation. They are still touring and releasing new material in 2018, albeit after a significant break. Talisman's brand of reggae has always had a light touch due in part to the influence of Brendan Whitmore's distinct saxophone style and Desmond (Lazarus) Taylor's vocals. Although Whitmore isn't in the reformed Talisman that sound is still in evidence on their 2017 album release *Don't Play With Fyah* (Sugar Shack Records). In 1981 Talisman released their seminal single 'Dole Age' and in 1982 they supported the Rolling Stones at Ashton Gate.

TARZAN THE HIGH PRIEST SOUND SYSTEM

Hector Thaws was known as Tarzan, hence the name of this sound system that ran during the late 60s and early 70s. He operated the system with his sons Roy and Rupert and (Natty) Lloyd Williams. It changed its name to Studio 17 in 1974 and ran until 1984 specialising in a rasta vibe. Roy Thaws is Adrian Thaws' father and Hector his grand father, Adrian Thaws is, of course better, known as Tricky.

THIS IS THE KIT

This Is The Kit is essentially singer songwriter Kate Stables and musicians Rozi Plain (bass), Neil Smith (guitar) and Jamie Whitby-Coles (drums). Their first album *Krulle Bol* in 2008 was produced by PJ Harvey collaborator John Parish. The folk-style sound and wistful lyrics have brought the band much critical acclaim from the likes of Elbow's Guy Garvey. In 2017 This Is The Kit released their fourth album *Monnshine Freeze*.

THOMAS BROOMAN CBE

Drummer with the Media, the Spics and Tesco Chainsaw Massacre in the late 70s and early 80s, Brooman was also one of the founders of the *Bristol Recorder*, an innovative and influential magazine and compilation LP in gatefold sleeve. It was through the *Recorder* that Brooman met Peter Gabriel and (with others) they went on to found the Womad festival which first took place in Shepton Mallet in 1982. In 2008, Brooman was awarded the CBE for services to music and charity. A fourth edition of the Bristol Recorder was released in 2018.

THREE CANE WHALE

The ability of this three-piece acoustic band to create images of landscapes through their music is truly astonishing. According to an *Observer* review 'the aroma of muddy eaves and old nettles is almost tangible'. Three Cane Whale are Alex Vann (mandolin, bowed psaltery, bouzouki, zither, banjo, dulcimer), Pete Judge (trumpet, cornet, dulcitone, harmonium, lyre, glockenspiel, tenor horn) and Paul Bradley (acoustic guitar, miniature harp). Their first eponymous album was chosen by 6 Music's Cerys Matthews as one of her top five modern folk albums, and their second album *Holts And Hovers* was *fRoots* magazine Editor's Choice Album of 2013, one of the *Observer's* "Hidden Gems Of 2013", and one of *Acoustic Guitarist* magazine's 20 Essential Folk Albums. The band's third album, *Palimpsest*, was recorded at Real World Studios in Wiltshire, produced by Portishead's Adrian Utley, and released in January 2016.

TORMENT

Psychobilly stars Torment were big news on the European festival circuit and in London at venues such as the Klub Foot, but rarely played their home town. Formed by Simon Brand (guitar, vocals), Kevin Haynes (drums) and Sean Holder (slap bass) in 1985. Tony Biggs and then Simon Crowfoot replaced Sean Holder and Torment released a series of highly rated albums and EPs including *Psyclops Carnival* (1986), *The Mystery Men EP* (1987), *Three's A Crowd* (1987), *Round The World* (1989) and *Hypnosis* (1990). Simon Brand died in 1994.

TRICKY

Tricky (Adrian Thaws) did not have a settled childhood. He's on record as saying: 'I've been through a lot. I've been moved around from family to family, never stayed in one house from when I was born to the age of 16. I'm not normal. It's got a lot to do with my upbringing. Staying somewhere for three years then going off for three years. My uncles being villains.

Tricky.

All that stuff. I've got quite a dysfunctional family, for some reason, in my family, the mothers always give the kids to the grandmothers'. Unsettled also describes Tricky's music. Brooding, dark often full of whispered menace and alienation, it snatches lyrical and musical references from many sources and layers them around bass-heavy beats.

Tricky's roots are in the Knowle West council estate but he was soon a regular fixture at the hip-hop parties of the early 80s in St Paul's where he hung out with the Wild Bunch and later with fellow Knowle Westerners and Merrywood schoolmates Fresh 4. He rapped with Massive Attack on *Blue Lines* and dueted with 3D on 'Karmacoma' on the *Protection* album. Famously, it's said that Tricky met Martina Topley-Bird when she was sitting on the wall of the house he was sharing with Mark Stewart of the Pop Group. She was having a fag break while revising for GCSEs at Clifton College and she went on to become the voice of his first album and the mother of their daughter Mazy.

That first album was *Maxinequay* – a reference to Tricky's late mother. Released in 1995, it peaked at number three in the UK Album Charts and went Gold. Since then he's released 12 albums, worked on a variety of side projects including films and remained staunchly and brilliantly unsettled.

UD4 CREW

The Ultimate Dynamic 4 Crew were a leading hip-hop force on the house party scene between 1983-1988 and also played out at the Dug Out, Moon Club and Granary. They comprised

Zion, Healer MC, Spider and The General (widely regarded as the best scratch DJ in town).

UNIQUE STAR SOUND SYSTEM

Unique Star sound system was born in 1989, an alias of Jah Lokko. Both sounds used the same speaker boxes and the same crew but operated in different genres and with different pre-amps. Unique Star are renowned for their stage at St Paul's Carnival, they have been hosting the City Road stage for more than 30 years.

VICE SQUAD

Vice Squad were from the fringes of Bristol – singer Rebecca Bond (Beki Bondage) came from Frampton Cotterell and Shane Baldwin (drums), Dave Bateman (guitar) and Mark Hambly (bass) from Kingswood/Hanham. Like many of their punk counterparts they formed a band in reaction to the boredom, conservatism and casual violence that ruled the suburbs.

They formed in 1978, the second generation of punk, and according to Baldwin were inspired by the moment that he and Bateman first listened to 'God Save The Queen' by the Sex Pistols in the back room of Bateman's house. Vice Squad played their first gig at Bristol University's Anson Rooms on April 12, 1979 but only played another six gigs for the next 18 months. They set up the Riot City label with Simon Edwards of Heartbeat Records and released their debut single 'Last Rockers' in 1981. John Peel famously opened his radio show every night for a week with 'Last Rockers' and the initial pressing of 1,500 copies sold out in a week. It went on the sell 22,000 copies and spent almost 40 weeks in the UK Indie chart, reaching number seven. The follow-up, 'Resurrection', reached number four, and the band undertook a tour supporting UK Subs. In 1981, the band signed to EMI (on their Zonophone subsidiary), prompting criticism from many within the DIY punk scene. Their first album, *No Cause For Concern*, was released in late 1981, reaching number 32 in the UK Album Chart. A second album followed in 1982, and the band embarked on a tour of the United States and Canada. On returning from the US, Bondage announced that she was leaving the band. She went on to front Ligotage and later Beki and the Bombshells, and, without her, Vice Squad were dropped by EMI. The new line-up featured new singer Lia and included the band's manager Mark 'Sooty' Byrne on second guitar. They signed with Anagram Records, and recorded a session for David Jensen's BBC radio show. Indie hits continued with singles such as 'Black Sheep' and 'You'll Never Know', but sales dwindled, and the band split up in 1985. Dave Bateman died in 2007.

WAY OUT WEST

Way Out West are producers Nick Warren and Jodie Wisternoff who previously performed as Tru Funk Posse with younger brother Sam and recorded with Smith & Mighty. Warren and Wisternoff pioneered a breakbeat/progresive house style and began releasing singles in 1994. Several of these were indie and club hits and in 1996 their single 'The

Gift' scored mainstream success when it reached number 15 in the UK Singles Chart. Way Out West have been releasing material ever since, most recently their fifth studio album *Tuesday Maybe* which came out in June 2017.

WAYNE HUSSEY

Wayne Hussey is from Coalpit Heath near Yate and went to the Ridings School in Winterbourne where he played in a band called Humph. But he's better known as one of the originators of goth with Dead Or Alive, the Sisters Of Mercy and the Mission.

WILD BUNCH

Wild Bunch were one of the original Bristol hip-hop posses and formed in the early 80s. The key members were MC Nellee Hooper, 3D, DJ Milo, Willy Wee and Daddy G. Tricky also rapped with the Wild Bunch. They signed to 4th & Broadway and released two 12-inch singles, 'Tearin' Down The Avenue' and 'Friends And Countrymen'. They then went on a tour of Japan, but it was badly organised and 3D left early. After recovering from the Japan experience 3D and Daddy G teamed up with Mushroom to form Massive Attack who released the seminal *Blue Lines* album in 1991 featuring Tricky. Tricky also appeared on Massive Attack's second album *Protection* which was produced by Nellee Hooper, who became one of the most sought-after producers in the business working with artists including Soul ll Soul, Bjork, Madonna, Smashing Pumpkins, U2 and Gwen Stefani.

YOLANDA CARTER

Singer with country/soul outfit Phantom Limb who formed in 2005 and eventually split up in 2013. Yolanda Carter toured as singer with Massive Attack and more recently has been exploring gospel music as a solo project.

YOUNG ECHO

This experimental collective of 11 artists and producers are taking drum and bass, dub and electronic music in unusual bass-heavy directions. Contributors to the Young Echo project include Jabu, Kahn, Vessel, Bogues, Manonmars, Ishan Sound, Neek, Ossia, Chester Giles, Rider Shafique and Gorgon .

Although this list is quite big, it's not definitive. We'll be updating it during and after the M Shed exhibition.

A BRISTOL TOP 40

● ● ● ● ● ●

ARTIST	TRACK	RELEASE DATE	LABEL
Acker Bilk	Stranger on the Shore	1961	Columbia Records
Andy Sheppard	May Song	2009	ECM Records
Beak>	Mono /Kenn	2012	Invada
Beth Rowley	Nobody's Fault but Mine	2008	Universal
Black Roots	Bristol Rock	1981	Nubian
Blue Aeroplanes	Jacket Hangs	1990	Ensign
Brilliant Corners	Brian Rix	1987	SS20
Cortinas	Defiant Pose/ Independence	1977	Step Forward
David And Jonathan	Lovers of the World Unite	1966	Columbia
Flynn & Flora	Dream of You	1994	Independent Dealers
Fred Wedlock	Oldest Swinger in Town	1980	Coast
Fresh 4	Wishing on a Star	1989	10
Gary Clail	Human Nature	1991	On-U-Sound
George Ezra	Budapest	2014	Columbia
Jaguar	Axe Crazy	1982	Neat
Joker	Digidesign	2009	Hyperdub
Julio Bashmore	Battle For Middle You	2011	PMR
K*ners	Bristol Grammar	2013	Forward Ever
Krust	Warhead	2007	V-Cycle
Massive Attack	Unfinished Sympathy	1991	Wild Bunch/Circa

ARTIST	TRACK	RELEASE DATE	LABEL
Maximum Joy	Silent Street	1981	Y
Onslaught	Killing Peace	2007	Candlelight
Ossia	Red X	2015	Blackest Ever Black
Peverelist	Roll With The Punches	2007	Punch Drunk
Pigbag	Papa's Got A Brand New Pigbag	1981	Y
Pinch	Quawwli	2006	Planet Mu
Pop Group	She Is Beyond Good And Evil	1979	Radar
Portishead	Glory Box	1994	Go! Discs
Rip Rig & Panic	You're My Kind Of Climate	1982	Virgin
Rita Lynch	Beautiful Eyes	1991	Moles
Roni Size/Reprazent	Brown Paper Bag	1997	Talkin' Loud
Shanti Celeste	Make Time	2017	Idle Hands
Smith & Mighty	B line Fi Blow	2010	Punch Drunk Unearthed
Talisman	Dole Age	1981	Recreational
This Is The Kit	Moonshine Freeze	2017	Rough Trade
Tricky	Tricky Kid	1996	4th & Broadway
Vice Squad	Last Rockers	1981	Riot City
Way Out West	The Gift	1996	RCA
Wurzels	Combine Harvester	1976	EMI
Young Echo	Umoja	2013	Ramp

* Compiled by M Shed curators and research/advisory group.

FURTHER READING

Adge King Of The Wurzels by John Hudson (Bristol Books)

Art & Sound Of The Bristol Underground by Chris Burton and Gary Thompson (Tangent Books)

Bovver by Chris Brown (Blake Publishing)

Bristol Boys Make More Noise: The Bristol Music Scene 1974-1981 by Gill Loats and John Spink (Tangent Books/Bristol Archive Records)

Bristol Folk by Mark Jones (Bristol Folk Publications)

Court In The Act: Ashton Court Festival 1974-1992 by Richard Jones (Bristol Community Festival)

Fred Wedlock Funnyman Of Folk by John Hudson (Bristol Books)

Last Rockers: The Vice Squad Story by Shane Baldwin (ACM Retro)

My Festival Romance by Thomas Brooman (Tangent Books/BAR)

Naked Guide To Bristol by Gil Gillespie and Richard Jones (Tangent)

Punks On Scooters by Michael Salter (Tangent/BAR)

Recollections Of Jazz In Bristol compiled by Dave Hibberd (Fiducia)

Straight Outta Bristol by Phil Johnson (Hodder & Stoughton)

The Granary Club by Al Read (Broadcast Books)

The Saydisc & Village Thing Discography by Mark Jones (Record Press)

Wild Dayz, Photos by Beezer (Tangent Books)